THE UNAPOLOGETIC ADVOCATE

HOW AND WHEN TO ADVOCATE FOR YOUR CHILD'S NEEDS

SARAH LAMB

ISBN: 979-8-9867275-4-7 (paperback)

CONTENTS

This book is dedicated to every caregiver who is constantly working behind the scenes to make things better. Because of people like you, people like me are inspired to do more.

A special thank you to those who took the time to read this book before print. Your help was so appreciated.

1

WHY AN UNAPOLOGETIC ADVOCATE?

When I was about three quarters done with writing this book, I got a phone call. Someone on my pretty small list of Facebook friends had taken a screenshot of one of my posts and shared it. In that post, I expressed frustration at a situation my youngest son felt uncomfortable with. It was a very short post. I didn't go into all the details, but someone who knew me and understood his fear expressed sympathy and disbelief at what I'd said, agreeing it was crazy. However, an unknown person went sharing that picture around, (why, I have no idea!) and that's when I got the call.

I was accused, in a roundabout way, by someone I didn't know personally and never had done more than nodded or waved to, of not being proud of my community or of my child's school, because my son had this fear. I sat there feeling stunned. It was one of those phone calls where you feel you can hardly get words out, let alone think because you are so rattled by shock, numb with surprise, and have a near anger at being accused of something so unfair.

After I hung up, I replayed the phone call in my mind several times. And then...I smiled. I smiled because I realized something. A few years ago, I would have handled that phone call very differently.

I didn't say "I'm sorry". I didn't apologize for my opinion, for my concern, for my child's wanting to feel safe. I didn't.

I used, "It was not my intent to offend anyone" but I don't consider that an apology. It was a statement. I don't want to offend anyone, but if someone feels offended that my child feels uncomfortable, and scared, and not included due to a medical condition he has NO control over, then maybe that's their problem, and not mine.

Have you ever felt frustrated and unheard when it comes to your child's needs?

The concerning thing is when these children grow up without the help they needed, they become adults trying to navigate the world with these same problems or conditions. Only now, they are unsure how to take care of themselves when things like a full-time job, higher education, starting a family, buying a house, or all that other adult stuff shows up at once. Those are also the situations that as much as we'd like to do something, we parents can't help.

Over the last few years, I've adopted this unapologetic attitude when it comes to my children and their medical and educational needs. I want you to have it too. You shouldn't have to be sorry for ruffling someone's feathers to get what your child needs. You shouldn't have to apologize when your child is left out. You shouldn't have to feel like a burden, in the way, or anything else. Neither should your child.

There are many who will say life isn't fair, and that's just how it is. I'm the first to say, "Yeah, it's not fair." But you know what? **Fairness and inclusiveness are two different things.** This isn't a book about fairness. It's a book about advocating for the care your child needs, be it with their education, their medical needs, or around friends or family. It's seeing their needs are met and they are included. Being inclusive doesn't take much more work, but being heard is what you are advocating for and that's usually the tough part.

You should be an unapologetic advocate and teach your child to be the same. Things won't get better until there are more of us who are unapologetic when it comes to seeing needs met.

Whether you are new to advocating for your child, or a seasoned caregiver who is looking for some new ideas and approaches, as well as some encouragement, this book is for you. As you move forward, I'll start off by briefly covering:

- What advocacy is

- How to do it

- The importance of communicating the right way

- Teaching your child to be a self-advocate

Next, you'll find information about how to advocate for your child in the following situations:

- At school

- In medical settings

- With friends

- Around family

Each section is broken down with common situations and what you need to look for and ask about. You'll also learn the importance of IHP, IEP, and 504 Plans, what they are, and how to get them. If traditional school isn't working, you'll also learn how your child's special services might not be cut off, and what options you may have to continue those in a home setting.

You'll learn the importance of having a support team for your child, and how to start building one. There is some spillover from one section to the next, but I've tried to lay it out logically, and in simple to understand language with short sections because you may not have time to wade through a long book, or might need to quickly refer to a particular section before a meeting.

At all times, remember, I am not a medical professional or giving any legal advice. I'm giving *Mom Advice*, chatting friend to friend. If you need medical, legal, or some other professional advice, please seek out a local (to you) professional. Additionally, if you or your child witness or know about a behavior that could endanger someone's life, such as sexual abuse, substance abuse, acting suicidal, or considering violence toward others, that is not the time to advocate. That is the time to call the authorities for help. This book is intended only for the day-to-day situations that arise with educational, medical, or relationship needs.

You've got this. Ready to start becoming unapologetic?

2

INTRODUCTION

Low quality schools. A child who needs a non-traditional classroom setting. Medical needs like: diabetes, food allergies, ADHD, POTS, long covid. Physical difficulties. Dyslexia. Autism. Acrodysostosis or other physical disabilities. Compromised immune systems. Mental disabilities. Learning disabilities. Or one (or more) of dozens of other common or uncommon needs that your child has. Invisible or visible needs.

These all have one thing in common, and that is that at one point or another you have likely had to advocate for what your child needs. Unfortunately, I'm sure you have also realized that being a parent or a caregiver and having to advocate never stops. You are always advocating for inclusiveness; you are always advocating for medical care. You are always advocating to make sure that your child gets the same education as others and that both you and they are taken seriously when there is a problem.

The thing is, it's not just a child with a special need who may require advocating. A child with no other "problems", at some time or another, is going to need to be advocated for. It could be because your school district just isn't doing good enough. It could be because you see your child struggling, and you don't know why. Your child might not be a traditional learner and needs an innovative approach. Maybe your child has concerns or fears (like peer pressure or bullying) and no one will listen at school or at the doctor's office. You'll be able to use some of these tips for that child as well, or share them with a friend who is searching for help on how to get what their child needs.

The focus of this book is to encourage and help and guide those of you who need to advocate but don't know how, or maybe just need to know you aren't alone. You don't want to draw the spotlight on yourself, you don't want to risk a child feeling embarrassed, you don't want to cause problems in the school or with family members or with a doctor. I totally get that. But what I also know is unless you are that squeaky wheel looking for the grease, you are not going to be taken seriously most of the time. Unless someone lives your life every single day, they absolutely do not understand your journey and your child's journey and what has to be done for them and the care that they need.

Advocacy, especially self-advocacy, is very important to me. There have been many times, even as an adult, I have let my own needs be overlooked when it came to medical or education situations. However, when my children began to have special medical and education needs at an older age, it was incredibly frustrating, painful, and upsetting to watch as they just were not getting the education they deserved or the medical care they needed.

I decided enough was enough. I spoke a little bit louder about what was needed. This is not to say this action has not had its growing pains. Absolutely it has. So many times things you are doing to ensure inclusiveness for your child falls under the radar. It's a role that seems almost at times as if you are an undercover agent. Quite a bit is being done on the sly and no one knows that it's you doing it.

While I don't think anyone should have to broadcast what they do to help others, it has been hurtful over the years for people to think that I don't participate in helping out in this situation or that. I am helping, but often I'm behind the scenes making sure that it is not just my kid, but theirs as well I'm there for, if possible.

It's likely that you have felt that frustration as well in always having to go above and beyond. Maybe it's the donating. Maybe it's the volunteering. The endless phone calls or emails? Late nights researching and teaching yourself how to understand medical or legal journals as you dig for the information you know is there somewhere. Whatever it is, I want you to know that I see you.

I see your hard work. I know you're staying up late at night and I know you're researching websites looking for help for your child. I know you plaster that smile on your face and stop the sigh, as once again you explain why something needs to be done a particular way or share the same piece of information for the tenth time, even though that info is in a file in the asker's hand and they just didn't take the time to read it. Does any of that sound familiar?

In this stretch of your life, I can't promise that dealing with your child's medical or educational difficulties will get easier, but I can promise that as you advocate more, and as they learn to self-advocate for themselves, that aspect will become easier. You might always be in that role of the background support person. The invisible wallflower that no one sees except to point a critical finger at. That does not change what you do though, and the significance of it. That does not change the fact that you are amazing and incredible and that you are doing a good job.

Being an advocate or self-advocate means there are a lot of things to think about that you might not have considered previously. That's what we're going to talk about in this book. We're going to hit some of the highlights where problems tend to occur the most.

How to use this book:

I've divided this book into multiple sections. While, of course, I would encourage you to read the entire thing, I know that sometimes you might just need a refresher on a topic. Perhaps you're getting ready to go to a family reunion and just want to focus on advocating for your child around family or friends. Because of this, there will be times you read a chapter and then flip over to another and you might feel like some of the information is the same. It could be some of the wording feels identical. That was done intentionally. Not to be redundant, but because of the fact there will be times I want you to know certain things. Use certain techniques. There are some things that will have a natural spill over from one topic to the next, but their importance is so great it must be repeated.

This book is not all inclusive. Each child is different, as are their needs. There's no way I could cover everything and it not be this monster sized and intimidating book. In being realistic...do you have time for that? Most of us don't! So, I've tried to make this as user friendly and as easily understood as possible, so that you and your child can benefit without wading through tons of fluff or fancy talk.

However, by touching on these common scenarios, these sections are designed to encourage and help you realize that you are not alone. Right this second, there are tens of thousands of people having to advocate for their children.

You can too.

I know this is hard. I know it's not fun. No one wants to rock the boat. But when you do, even if you capsize, you'll find out how strong you are on the swim to shore.

There is so much power behind knowing that you are not alone. I want each of you reading this to know that you are not alone. Everything you do has a ripple effect. The advocacy you do today helps another child tomorrow. And another the day after. Let's work together to make sure every child's needs are met physically, mentally, educationally, and emotionally.

There may be times you stop and ask yourself: "Is this worth it?" This is you, learning what's small and unimportant, and what needs pursuing. This is a decision only you and your child know. It's that gut feeling telling you to go after that thing or let it drop. But when it's time to get action, that's what this book is for.

It's time to not take no for an answer. And if no is all you get, it's time to learn how to walk away.

PART ONE

Learning About Advocating

3

BEING DIFFERENT

I want to open with a story. I recently was scrolling on Facebook and saw a mother had started a post. She said her six-year-old had asked why he was so different. So, so, many others were talking about that in the comments. Each said the same. Their kid wondered about it as well, and they hated that question. They were miserable that their kid felt different.

Totally, I get that. I do. But what was missing from that post? It was glaringly obvious to me. The fact that out of dozens of moms replying, not one said that different is okay. There was no reassuring the kid that there wasn't anything wrong with them. And that bothered me.

When a child feels left out, we should advocate for them. Sometimes, though, that advocacy needed is a reminder for that child, not just others around them. My reply to the post was that after giving a hug, I hoped the mother reminded her child how if we were all the same it would be so boring! How, yes, there were things that couldn't be done in their particular situation, but there were so many more that could be!

A medical condition doesn't get to say who someone is. A learning disability doesn't define you. A difficult environment doesn't get to determine your destiny. Only you, the person, get to do that. I then asked another question...what if. What if he wasn't different? What if it is the others he meets who are?

Being or feeling different allows you to see things from an alternate perspective. It allows the growth of empathy, of awareness, of positivity if you nurture those traits. However, without support or encouragement, it can also bring depression, a sense of isolation, and negativity.

Maybe you aren't here because your child has a medical need. Maybe it's education that concerns you. The school isn't helping like they should. You feel like your child is having difficulties in an area, be it with learning or emotionally. School has become a chore that no one likes. I'm going to touch on that later, in a small section to share that it's okay to have these difficulties and work toward reducing them.

As you read these pages, I hope that instead of feeling dejected and overwhelmed, you feel the positivity I am trying to put into this book. That instead of feeling defeated, you feel energized and fired up. Ready to make the change. Ready to be the change.

Change is what advocacy is. And advocacy is change. It's pointing out a need, showing a flaw in the way things are done, and a new way to do things. Advocating doesn't just help in the now, but also in the future.

By your actions today, you might be only helping one, but a few years from now, those deeds may have helped hundreds. Isn't that an amazing idea?

4

DO IT SCARED!

Just after an upsetting situation of any kind, we all feel a bit of uncertainty, to say the least. Life is very different. Things we did last month, things we ate yesterday, things we planned to do next week—no matter what it is, it all feels different, and foreign, and *dangerous*.

There are a lot of phone calls, a lot of new worries, a lot of what ifs. A lot of the wobbly voice and tears and absolute overwhelm and confusion. How are you going to manage to do all of this? At the same time, there's the need to learn more about this condition or concern, or even recognize the fact that what you've been doing just isn't working, and it's time to find a new way. A way to educate yourself and get every bit of knowledge that you can to learn how to not just manage or navigate these new challenges, but also how to find the good, and help yourself, your child, or your family member. You need to learn how to thrive. How to create positivity and make your community stronger or more aware.

Right after a medical diagnosis, none of that seems possible, but I promise, it is. In small ways, great changes happen. Think about a seed you might plant in your garden. It's so tiny. But planting it isn't an insignificant act. That little seed has a great change in front of it. You do too. But no doubt about it, there are plenty of tears, wobbly voices, and worry along the way.

This same thing happens when your child is struggling in school. Maybe it's the method of learning, the environment, the teachers, or their peers. Whatever it is, you know something has to be done because your child doesn't deserve to suffer like they have been.

That tight throat, the tears trying to come out, the heart pounding in terror and the feelings of anger, overwhelm, and worry are yours too. But you've got to do it anyway, right?

That's called doing it scared. Doing what you need to do because it must be done. And doing it because you, or someone you love, is depending on you to do it.

This is the smallest section of the book, but it's a mighty one! As you read this book, sprinkled through the pages you're going to learn how to do things when you are scared. Do things when you are tired, overwhelmed, or at the very, very last little bit in your metaphorical battery.

One day, I promise you, it's going to get a little easier. And you're going to start seeing changes made in your small world. Changes because of you and this diagnosis or decision that you keep coming back to.

So where to start when you are learning to do things through this worry and fear? If possible, it helps to remove the emotion from a situation. Remember, you, your child, or your loved one are not their diagnosis or difficulty. They are still them. This thing that has happened is a worry, yes, but it's also a problem. And all problems have a solution. It might not be a complete solution. It's also not always one we are fully happy with, but there is always a way to move forward and work on improving the situation.

The first step is to advocate.

5

What Is an Advocate?

Are you familiar with this word? It's time for it to become a part of your everyday vocabulary. An advocate is a person who speaks up for someone who can't or has trouble doing it. A parent is an advocate because most children don't get the respect that they deserve when trying to speak about their health problems or difficulties in school. If you've heard the phrase patient advocate, that's usually someone in a position at a medical facility who is there on behalf of the patient to get them the best care possible, or whatever it is they need, so that they can get the proper care, like if an insurance company is refusing to cover a suggested treatment.

Self-advocacy is when someone at any age speaks up for themselves. Any sort of advocacy requires confidence and courage because it can be a difficult thing, and it can be really overwhelming or frightening to speak up. No one likes to feel they are causing a problem or being a disturbance or a troublemaker. A lot of people don't like to stand out; they don't want to be seen as different, or as needing help in a situation. There's no shame in needing help though, and there's no shame in needing an advocate if there is something you're not able to do yourself.

Advocates can appear in many work or school or medical situations. Part of a union at work? Chances are very high you have a union advocate, though they might be called a union representative. Advocates have been around a long time, and in many environments. You can even find them locally or online by a quick search. Many will meet with you to assist in a difficult situation.

The thing about being an advocate, though, is it's not always popular. It's not the majority opinion being advocated, it's not always what everyone wants to hear. It's something that you have to do with that burning desire, that intense passion, that longing for inclusion or to be taken seriously, and you have to walk through those flames even when things aren't fun. Even when people might give you a weird look or whisper little comments. Or leave Facebook comments and suggest that you're an idiot for trying to go against the status quo.

In an era where inclusion is so important for so many topics, it seems strange that medical inclusion is often overlooked and often ignored. Think about how many times your eyes go across the newspaper headlines and see someone who has tragically passed away or now is in stage four cancer because they couldn't get a doctor to take them seriously. They couldn't get the tests or the help that they needed until it was too late.

Or maybe it was the opposite. They gave up because they thought the doctors knew best. They were told it was all in their head, that they didn't fit the statistic of having a problem, and so they were fine. Go home.

Pause for a second...have you ever had someone tell you that? You knew they were wrong, didn't you? But their words made you feel otherwise. It's time to stop that!

There are a few, oh so few, who you'll also read about. They didn't give up. From place to place they went, looking for help because they were trying so hard to advocate for themselves. Something wasn't right and they knew it. They also knew if they kept looking, even though it was hard, they'd find the help or solution that was out there. That's where you need to be.

It's not just for medical situations. The same can be said for education. The school knew best. Others were right and the worrier's gut was just being wonky and they should ignore it. Have you ever thought that? Worried about that? Have you ever doubted yourself and wondered if your instincts were wrong? Were they, though? Maybe sometimes things worked out in your favor, but how many times have you wished that you'd just listened to your gut.

Think back to other headlines you've seen, articles you've read about kids. Bullying; threats against other students? Difficulty in class, but without any one thing that pinpointed as to why? How often did someone try to get help but were ignored? How often did they give up, thinking they didn't matter? *They* didn't matter?

How many people might still be with us if someone had just listened?

It's hard to stand up for what you believe in, but this book is going to help you learn how to do that and how to help your child learn to self-advocate. Like anything else, the more you advocate, the easier it gets. It becomes second nature. Even better, one day you'll find that those little comments and those eye rolls and the doctor or the teacher who ignores you gets a little bit easier to manage.

Sometimes it feels like we are in an era where unless you are a person who *is someone* that anything you suggest is going to be wrong. Maybe it's impostor syndrome you are feeling. Or maybe it's that you have tried to say something in the past and got a negative result, so trying to speak now is uncomfortable and upsetting and unsettling.

Here's something interesting but unexpected about that. When you advocate, even if it's for someone else or for something small, say a new way of doing something that's only been done one way for a decade, you'll find those who were too unsure or scared to speak up will tell you afterwards they appreciated you voicing your thoughts. I used to be that way myself. Sitting, hoping someone would say what I wanted to say at a PTO meeting, in a group of people, wherever. Not wanting to be the one who was looked at. Called out. In the spotlight. All because what if they didn't like what I said?

As time went on, I realized that fear tries to prevent you from doing what you should. It holds you back from making progress. After all, if you do that thing, fear doesn't exist anymore, right? You've just kicked it to the curb and have no more use for it. Fear doesn't want that! Just as importantly, I also realized if I don't speak up for myself, my children, or others, who will?

So, let's keep going to learn more about advocacy, starting with self-advocacy.

6

SELF-ADVOCACY

Does anyone else cringe when the phone rings and it's from your child's school or doctor? Every time for me. I get nervous, my chest tightens, my stomach has at least a few dozen butterflies startled into a sudden aerial show.

This particular day, it was a call from school and I was told my son had possibly been exposed to one of his food allergens, but they were not sure. He seemed fine, but they'd like me to pick him up because he was nervous and shaken. As I left work, I wondered what the rest of the story was. After I hugged my kid, looked him over, and we walked toward the car, he told me what happened.

And I was so proud of him.

I'm going to back up a second. My children are both boys, but well behaved and respectful of adults. They listen well and generally are pretty polite. That includes waiting until someone is done talking to speak.

My youngest told me they were in music class. They had been required to put hand sanitizer on before entering the class. He does, then looks over. A picture of a fruit that he didn't recognize was on the bottle. He stood there, panicking, wanting to wash his hands because he has a coconut allergy and was scared that picture was of a coconut. He then tried to read the bottle, but there were so many words, and so many long words. It was impossible for him to do it. He raised his hand but wasn't called on. He was filled with worry and tried to call the teacher's name. She didn't hear him over the other children. So, loudly, he shouted, "I touched my allergen and I'm going to DIE!"

Now, obviously, that might have been a little drastic. He wasn't feeling any symptoms of a reaction, but the point is, he knew he had possibly been exposed to something dangerous and it was up to him to get help. At that moment, he had the teacher's attention. She looked at the hand sanitizer, didn't see coconut, but sent my son up to the nurse.

The nurse wasn't there, which is why I was called. Better safe than sorry, and I agreed. But I was so proud of him because we've talked many times over the years about the importance of self-advocating and he did it. He told me how scared he was. Scared of possibly being exposed and having an allergic reaction, and even more scared of the teacher getting mad at him. After, again, telling him how proud I was of him, I asked, "What made you not scared?"

He thought about it for a while, then said, "I was scared. But I had to do it. I had to count on me."

And that is what self-advocacy is. It's standing up for yourself, even if there might be consequences because you need to do it.

So how to self-advocate? For an adult or for a child, it might take different forms, but the result is still the same. Self-advocating is standing up for yourself when no one else can or will do it for you. In the case of my son's story, he was at school, and knew he was responsible for his medical needs. That included advocating for himself to be heard and get the care he needed.

Maybe your child also has a medical need. Maybe they have an educational need, and when it's time for something in class, they know they need to be accommodated or helped in a particular way. What if that doesn't happen? What do they do? This is where it's so important to teach your child self-advocacy. With a teacher to student ratio allowed in our state of 1:25, your child can, and possibly will, slip through the cracks, no matter how well-meaning the school or teacher is.

I'd like to break this down a little more, because obviously, self-advocating is based on age and maturity level, but also what the needs of that individual are. A child who has learning needs is going to have different ways of expressing self-advocacy from the child with food allergies, diabetes, or with asthma. However, though the need might be different, as could be the style of approach, one thing is the same—there is a time they will need to self-advocate. This skill is critical to have, and the sooner it's developed the better.

Of course, a medical or educational need can happen at any time and any age, but as this book is designed to help in multiple situations and ages, I'm going to start from an early age to share age-appropriate suggestions for teaching your child to advocate for themselves. Even if you have an older child, start with this first section. The tips are very helpful, and a perfect starting point for anyone new to whatever challenges they are facing and need to advocate for.

7

TODDLER AND PRESCHOOL AGE ADVOCACY

Advocacy can start at a young age. So does awareness of a child's body. It's important to teach your child to think about how they feel. This can be done in everyday situations. If they fall and scrape their knee, you can say, "I see you have hurt your knee!" If they have a cold or seasonal allergies, you can say, "I see how stuffy your nose is!" Recognizing the different body parts and the discomfort they feel is a great first step to developing body awareness. They then know what feels normal and what doesn't.

Perhaps if your child struggles with numbers, or mobility, or sees letters switched around, your questions might be, "I see how hard you are trying to do this. It looks like it might be difficult. Can you tell me what is making this hard?" Just a simple question, a statement. No judgment. Just awareness of their difficulty and leaving the conversation open so they can ask or demonstrate help is needed, and explain what the problem might be, such as the letters keep moving, it's hard to grasp the crayon, or they can't hear the instructions said.

Knowing that others also have the same challenges as we do is important. Books, cartoons, and of course, meeting other children who have to manage the same difficulty they do can not only model good ways of self-advocacy but also help your child to see that others also have the same struggles and that they aren't different. Even if your child never gets to meet these others in person, sometimes just knowing they aren't alone makes all the difference.

If your child needs a medical device, include them in the responsibility of checking to be sure they have it before leaving home. Extend that to showing the proper care of the item and the place it should always be kept while at home. Create the habit, and as they are older, it's second nature. Take opportunities to remind them of the importance of this device, how it works, the way to take care of it, and if an adult needs to help with its use. If you need a visual reminder, consider something that goes in the front door like a sign or a custom-made magnet you can see before you leave, or something that's inside of your car.

Show your child those who can and should help and answer questions. Point them out and remind your child to look for these helpers if you are not there. These helpers can be a trusted family member, a babysitter or child care provider, preschool teacher, or doctor. Sometimes just knowing who will help or who will answer questions if they arise is enough to give your child the confidence in starting to self-advocate.

However, just like you might encourage your child to be familiar with a needed medical device or what assistance is needed in the classroom, if there is also something your child should not have, take opportunities to point it out and explain in simple language why they cannot have it. Use simple language such as "That could hurt you" or "That is okay for Mama, but that is not okay for you" or "When you do this, your teacher needs to help you".

8

ELEMENTARY AGE ADVOCACY

Once a child starts school, there is a lot more to worry about. In the section devoted to schools, you'll learn a little more about some of the options available so you and other adults can support your child. However, the fact of the matter is once your child is in school, they have to learn to take care of themselves in that setting. Yes, even at a young age and despite having an IEP, IHP, or 504 Plan (which I will explain more about later in the book).

Teachers and other adults, while usually well-meaning and doing their best, often do not know if a child needs help or not, especially if there is no known or established need. Between the child who always needs a bandaid, the one who always has a stomachache, and the one who is a little too mischievous for their own good, teachers have their hands full. They also have a lesson to teach, likely twenty other children in the classroom, if not more, and it is easy, even with the IEP, IHP, or 504 Plan for a child's needs to slip through the cracks.

Obviously, there are instances, especially when it comes to young children or those with mental or severe educational needs, someone cannot take care of themselves in this way. It is then the adult who may need to be hyper aware of the situations the child is in and have more of a frequent check in with those providing care or education for the child. Typically if that is the case, your child is in a smaller classroom, with a teacher to student ratio that is more favorable for their success.

For those who can be aware of their needs and surroundings, it is important for your child to have the knowledge of what they should or should not be expected to do, as well as of any accommodations that have been granted for things such as school work, field trips, food used in classroom lessons, lunches, physical education, and transportation.

By your child being aware of what they should expect for those topics, if something seems off, if it seems different from how it should be or how it usually is, they are more likely to speak out, possibly preventing frustration, exclusion, or something more serious.

While this is a child-by-child situation, I have always included my children in age-appropriate conversations with their doctors and the school when it comes to their needs, and made sure they were given the opportunity to ask any questions they had. I've also encouraged my children to answer the questions at their well-check visits, including those about if they have any allergies or other medical history things the doctor needs to know. My reasoning? Sure, it would be easier, maybe even quicker, to do it on my own. However, for me, this is a temporary thing to deal with, to talk about. For them? A lifetime. They need to be comfortable both talking about and familiarizing themselves with the language of their medical diagnosis and history, so as they grow into adulthood they are equipped to care for their needs.

When thought about in that perspective, I've also always felt strongly about teaching them how to use and care for any medical device, even if it is small, especially anything that may be potentially life-saving. For many, they will need these devices for the rest of their lives. As a parent and caregiver, it is my job to help them understand how to use and care for whatever they need, as well as how to self-advocate, so that one day, it's second nature not just to them, but it increases the awareness of others around them.

Sometimes none of this is easy. It can be hard to speak up, and children are often shy around those they don't know. That's not a bad thing! However, learning how and when to speak for themselves is important. It can start small to let their comfort level grow. You might not just want to throw your child into it, saying, "Okay! Here we are! You do the talking today!" That wouldn't work for my kids, anyway! They'd freeze in fear! A little advance notice is often valuable. Let them know that you are so proud of how capable they are, and you are going to help them learn how to do this new thing, and that tomorrow, they are going to do it.

For example, next time you go out to eat, have your child order their food. At first, they might stumble, but before long, they'll be quite confident in ordering chicken nuggets, French fries, and a chocolate milk, please.

9

TEEN ADVOCACY

Teens can be hard. They come in the listening and careful type, and the rebellious, my way sort, and everything in between. The difficulty of having a child with a special need in these older years is once middle school hits, schools seem to shut you out. They expect children to be miniature adults and able to take care of things on their own.

That's great in theory. But, for example, my teen needing epipens. The school doesn't want him to self carry, and the lockers are not secure. Anyone can just jiggle the door and it opens. Combine kids wanting to play around with someone else's things, food in the classrooms, and the nurse's office very far away in a large school, that's a problem for kids with food allergies, especially my oldest, who developed one at age twelve, and finds his throat closes within a minute. There's not enough time to recognize the problem and get treatment if the epipens are not with him.

This is where self-advocacy is so important. Teens need to recognize potential problems. For example, needing an inhaler before or after PE, or needing to change for PE or a sport while wearing an insulin pump. Or maybe carrying books and taking notes with the use of only one arm. Perhaps it's that they need to take medicine at the same time each day. What of a child who needs a mobility device? How can they navigate stairs or crowded hallways? What about the seating in a classroom? Is it where they can easily maneuver?

On the educational side, is someone supposed to read test questions to them? Are they allowed extra time during an exam or a calculator in math? They need to be aware of each thing that should happen, so when that aid isn't there for them, they can speak up to have it.

Once a teen has identified the potential problems in their day, they can work with the school, coaches, and other caregivers to find a solution. There is always a solution, it just might need to be creative. If the teen finds that the solution isn't working, they need to feel empowered enough to speak up and say so.

If there is food in the classroom, they need to feel confident in saying, "Mrs. Jones, I'm allergic to that, and

I don't feel like I can concentrate on my work with Jack eating."

Or, they might need to say, "It's difficult for me to get from one classroom to the next because I have to move slower or need more clearance. Can I please leave a minute before everyone else does?"

It could also be as simple as saying, "Even with my glasses, I'm having trouble seeing. Can I move closer?" or "I keep trying to understand that math problem, but I can't. Will you please help me learn a different way?"

Teens are also at that age they don't like to draw attention to themselves. But this is why self-advocacy is even more important. Teach them it's not a big deal to need to ask these things. Make it normal, and the discomfort reduces if not vanishes. Everyone has something they need help with or do differently. Normalizing this fact, as well as helping them to realize they are NOT a bother when they need something is incredibly important.

Recently, Christmas Eve no less, my teen ate something he's eaten many times before. In fact, out of the same package he'd had just a few days earlier. This time, though, his stomach started hurting. His chest got tight. He was struggling to breathe. I was ready, but I wanted him to make his choice before I made it for him. He didn't want to be a bother. It was Christmas Eve! Within a few minutes, he was supposed to Zoom with his grandparents and open Christmas gifts with his little brother. We talked for just a few seconds, and he made the choice to use the epipen. With shaking hands, he used it (I monitored) while I called 911. He was worried about causing others to be inconvenienced, but understood the importance of self-advocating for what he needed in that moment. It was a hard choice he had to make, but the moment he started to feel better from the epinephrine, he was grateful he'd done it.

After all, solving a problem (for my son, using the epipen, going to the hospital for a few hours, and then coming home) is much better than struggling and experiencing the consequences that come with not getting the help you need (in this case, a more serious reaction or even death). While not every time of speaking up will be life or death, to a teen, it might feel just as uncomfortable. Just like anything else though, they more they feel comfortable making those good decisions for themselves, the easier it becomes.

As teens start to spend more time with peers, and less with their families, this self-advocacy plays a huge role. You want a child who feels confident in saying no to situations they don't feel comfortable in, no matter the type, knowing they have an adult fully supporting them in that decision. You also need that child prepared to take care of themselves, even in moments when they don't want to stop having fun, or they may miss out on something.

Encourage their tribe, that group of friends who will help or support your child. If those individuals are not at your child's school, make sure they still get to see them often. Build their support system. Sometimes knowing someone understands and doesn't think less of them for whatever challenge they have is all that is needed on a rough day.

10

YOUNG ADULT ADVOCACY

If your young adult has been self-advocating for years, it's likely they feel comfortable. If they are new to this, much of the same advice for teens can apply to them, if they are still in school. However, the older someone gets, the more they are expected to care for themselves, even if they still need help to navigate some situations.

If your young adult is planning to go away to school or get their first job, suggest that they think ahead of time about what things they might need accommodations on.

For someone with gastrointestinal problems, it might mean extra or longer restroom trips. Perhaps a delivery job or one where they are stuck at a register for hours at a time isn't a good choice. Maybe someone with a smoke, dust, and mold allergy should not be working in an outdoor setting or be roommates with a smoker.

Explore the options available, seek out the resources that schools and companies offer, and use them. They are provided for that reason. Colleges often have a person to contact for that, and sometimes the recruiter or high school counselor can help make those introductions. When it comes to jobs, you might be able to preview some of that information from the human resources department online, or call someone ahead of time to ask detailed questions or even stop by for a sly bit of reconnaissance.

One thing that might be helpful to remind your child is depending on the situation, the things they do now might not be permanent. Actions can be and are adjusted as time goes on and they learn better how to navigate the situation they find themselves in. Sometimes, it's better to err on the side of caution at first until they are familiar with the people and the place, and feel comfortable advocating for themselves.

11

OKAY, NOW WHAT?

It's important at any age to learn to ask for what is needed and not to feel bad for doing it. That leads us into the next topic. Being scared or uncomfortable about seeking help or standing out.

But first, a final word on teaching your children to self-advocate.

Children learn by example. They learn through experience. Encourage them to speak and be part of conversations. Be an example by advocating and being filled with facts, ideas, patience, and understanding, not getting upset and giving up because it's hard. Show the strength a powerful but respectful request can have. Let them see asking is not a weakness, and nothing to be ashamed of. Even if the result is not one you like, let them see you tried. And teach your child how and when to walk away.

Remember, always... fear is natural. And it's okay to feel fearful or worried about something, but don't let it stop you.

It's okay to be scared.

No matter the age, it's important that your child, or any other adult, understand that it is okay to be scared and it is okay to say no to something that doesn't make them feel comfortable. Even more importantly, it's okay to walk away from a situation that doesn't seem right. We'll talk more about that at the end of the book, but it's important as you learn to advocate and self-advocate that you and your child realize "no" is an acceptable word to use.

Often children want to please others and they want to please adults. They might engage in risky behavior because of that. Everyone wants to be liked, and seen as normal or cool. But sometimes they're too young to understand there are consequences from an action that are more dangerous than they realize. Think of a ball rolling across the street. A young child may only see the ball as a short distance away and rush to get it. A child who is older, and has more experience and knowledge, knows that cars frequently pass on the street. This child knows to pause and look before crossing, or the need to go with an adult in order to retrieve their ball.

That same behavior stays with a child as they grow in maturity and learn that some things, like crossing the road in front of the car as a dare, is a bad idea. Teach your child to listen to their gut but also to stand up for themselves. Standing for what is right, what is needed, inclusiveness, and for the safety of yourself or another is never a wrong thing to do.

12

WHEN TO SAY NO

This "no" is especially important in a school setting. Did you know that in many schools your child's principal has the right to question them privately, without you? And, depending on the school district, without you knowing? The Supreme Court labeled this idea "in loco parentis" which means instead of the parent or in place of the parent. That idea makes me uncomfortable, and it might also make your child feel scared. Picture that scenario; your child with someone who is supposed to be a trusted adult having a conversation about their health, their education, or an event that took place at school without you.

Would your child tell you about the conversation? Or would they assume the school told you? Your child may be under the impression that you knew the difficulties they were having because they had discussed it with another adult, one in a position of authority, who they assumed would tell you. Then, if you didn't take steps to help this situation, what would your child think? That you didn't care? That it wasn't really important?

It is these private conversations that often lead to other problems too, because your child may not feel confident enough in advocating for themselves. To be honest, at times they might not even be given an opportunity to do so. Many adults talk over children of all ages. Many adults also want to sweep incidents under the rug and pretend they didn't happen. Without an adult advocate, there is only the word of the school to say what took place or did not.

This same scenario happens in medical offices. I'm sure you've heard of doctor / patient confidentiality. You might be completely fine with that. There may be things that your child only wants to discuss with a therapist or doctor. However, be aware that anything they say, even something benign, could be kept from you.

Teach your child saying no isn't wrong. That if they feel put into a situation where they don't feel comfortable, or it doesn't seem fair and they can't get a word in edgewise, *stop talking*. Encourage them to say, and say firmly, that they won't talk without their parent / caregiver. It is their right. Just like it should be yours to be there to support your child and make sure they are protected during any potential private conversation with an adult.

From a young age, we teach our children about stranger danger. We tell them don't follow someone who says they've lost their puppy. Don't take candy from a stranger. Don't get into a car with anyone else, even if they say they are taking you to your parents. But we don't teach our children that sometimes it is okay to say no to an adult who is in an authoritative sort of position. It is important we let our children know that it is *always* okay to be polite and respectfully refuse to speak without their adult advocate if they feel they are in a situation where they cannot advocate for themselves.

Verbal communication isn't the only kind that happens. However, regardless of how you communicate, there are certain things you need to do. This next section will explain this more in depth.

13

COMMUNICATION

There will be many times you need to communicate regarding your child and their needs. Perhaps it's to a caregiver, a school, or a medical facility. Maybe it's your insurance company, a specific friend, or family member. There are many instances where you may need to speak with someone about your child and the way they have been treated or should be treated moving forward.

It will be important you communicate the right way. These tips and tricks will also aid your child when it comes to them self-advocating as a young adult, so as you model these tactics, they can learn how to communicate effectively with others.

While absolutely, you might be hopping mad, you can't (or rather, shouldn't!) show it unless it's a situation where your child's life was in danger. The logical, calm, well thought out responses to a situation get better results, and also make YOU look better. People are less likely to take the upset person seriously or help them; the angry person loses credibility, gets flustered, and it is incredibly easy to twist their words around and make them stumble over them so that they can't speak their thoughts. Even if you are completely justified in how you are feeling, it's just not a good idea to let your emotional side take over in the conversation.

But sometimes it takes a while for that cool head. And sometimes you just don't know what to say or how to say it. Maybe you get very nervous when talking to people. I know I do! You feel kind of flustered and you forget what you wanted to say or you let them make you feel like what you had to say wasn't important. Or perhaps like the French term *l'esprit d'escalier*, you are faced with the predicament of when you think up the perfect thing to say, but only after you've left the conversation. Though not as popular of a phrase in America, we would call it staircase wit—thinking of something to say, but only after it's too late.

Don't worry. I've got tips for you, and they are not only easy, but really step up your advocating game. Ready for them?

Take notes

It sounds so easy, doesn't it? Simply take notes. It's a little bit more involved in that, especially if you tend to be a household where there's never an ink pen around. Before having a conversation on the phone or in person, I encourage you to find a notepad and a pen and get ready to take notes. What kind of notes? Well, you might want to start with the date. Time is optional, but it might be helpful to have that down. Put on the person's name that you're speaking with. If it's easier, ahead of time briefly jot down your questions and then their answers up underneath, so you don't forget to ask all you wanted to know.

Or, if this is a conversation where you are just wanting to listen or you needed to return a call, then make brief notes as to what is said. While, of course, anything said on the phone is not a legal record unless it was recorded, your notes can often be helpful for you to refer back to.

In the case of a business, such as an insurance company, there might be an electronic file and it is possible that the person speaking on the other end will also be taking notes. If you are given a case number or a reference number, write that down as well. Those help your information to be pulled up quicker next time you speak to that place. Ask if there is someone else you need to follow up with and get that person's information. If someone is supposed to get back with you, ask when that is. That way, if it's been longer than expected, you can call yourself and follow up.

It's important not to assume that others will do the work of getting back with you. Often they don't. They get busy and put things off like we all do. However, when it comes to your child's needs, you have every right to follow up, if it's been longer than it should have been to get a response.

An important aspect of note taking, and one that we almost never think about until afterwards, is did we copy down the information correctly? Double check that email address or phone number before you hang up. Some numbers and letters sound so similar to each other it would be very easy to mistake a "S" for an "F" or "7" for an "11". Especially when distracted with something going on in the background or you have a poor call connection. And poor connections seem to be an extremely common thing when trying to make or take a phone call! Do they pay extra for that static or echoing that always seems to be on the line, I wonder.

The purpose of these notes is not just to prompt your memory, but just look at how much more empowered are you, when you can say, "Mr. Smith, we spoke about this June 14th, at 11:30am."

Best trick ever! Schedule your emails

Have you ever sent an email and a few minutes later thought ARGGGGGHHH I forgot to say this! You can't see it, but I'm raising my hand. That's me, all the time.

Until I learned I could *schedule* my emails! While that might not be an option for everyone, it does depend on who hosts your email, with Gmail, definitely that's an option.

It's incredibly easy to do, and just a few clicks later, you can choose what day and time you want your email sent, and your email will send it automatically. If you aren't familiar with this, or you wonder if your email uses scheduling, a quick Google will help you out!

What's so great about scheduling your email? Isn't the whole point to send that email and get a reply? Here are a few reasons you might want to schedule your emails:

- It gives you time to think about your reply

- It gives you a chance to add or remove something

- It makes you seem like you weren't in a hurry to reply

A bit more in depth about each of those.

It gives you time to think about your reply

Sometimes it's very important to think carefully before replying. There are facts to confirm, a hot temper to cool, and the practice of typing out a logical, polite reply when you just don't want to be those things.

The funny thing is...and you'll read more about that here in a moment, under *Read. And reread again.* is that often, that first instinctual reply isn't the best one you can send.

It gives you a chance to add or remove something

That doctor or teacher name you forgot but just came to your brain, the incident that happened a few weeks back that supports your concern, or the question you wanted to ask. What do these three things have in common? *L'esprit d'escalier.* The staircase wit. I'm not sure there's a human alive who doesn't suffer from this. Just after we hang up the phone, send the email, drive away...that's when we remember. Scheduling your emails lets you quickly go in and add that missing information. You don't have to schedule far. Even an hour ahead. But it creates a safety net for you.

On the other hand... once your cooler head prevailed, did you find you were perhaps harsher in a reply than you should have been? There's time to change it, unlike if you pressed send right away.

Most of us don't get a second chance in life to do something, but here, you are *creating* that second chance for yourself. It's a very powerful move in advocacy.

It makes you seem like you weren't in a hurry to reply

Sometimes it irritates me when someone wants a reply right away, or you feel that unspoken pressure to reply, without having everything you need to give a proper answer. That's often a tactic used against you deliberately. And how often, even if you reply right away, do you even hear back quickly? Or do you sit around, pacing, nervous and biting your nails, jumping at every notification on your phone?

There are some individuals who thrive on the power of putting pressure on others. This can be a method they employ to throw others off balance. If that's the case...business hours. Just because your phone or inbox dings doesn't mean you have to go running. Boundaries! I bet they've got them too.

Your life does not revolve around their impatient schedule. So, if they've got to wait until morning to get a reply to their email that doesn't need an urgent reply, that's what they have to do. Meanwhile, you already replied, it's just scheduled, so you aren't feeling stressed.

Reread. And reread again.

Sometimes I get an email or a text message and smoke practically comes out of my ears! I'm ready to pound out my reply and make sure that my side is seen, and seen correctly. Because I'm in the right...right? I'm justified in my anger and why isn't the other person knowing that?

But...what if I'm not?

Over the last year, I have made myself stop and wait a little before I reply. It's been a conscious action, and at times it's hard to do, but oh the benefits! I promise you, it's hard not to click that send button when you are angry, or feeling justified, worried, or upset, but trust me. You can still write all that you want to say, but communicate in a more efficient and effective way.

Here's what you do. Write it out. Write every bit of it. Or, say it in your head. I run through every single reply in my head and I let myself feel outraged and irritated, and then I go read the email again. Reading it, I start to type up my reply.

Doing this, I've noticed that many times I see the other person's message differently. As I read the message a second or third time, certain words pop up and grab my attention. Then, I now see *the other person's* concern, upset, or worry. I've come to realize that many times, their questions or comments aren't out of a place of anger, defensiveness, or rudeness. They are asking so many questions or sticking to scripted answers because they are worried. They don't want the liability, they've never been in a situation like this, they don't know how YOU will respond, or they feel in over their heads. Sometimes it is even genuine concern and a desire to help.

Now wait! I promise I'm not making this all about the other person. You might still be justified in a small part of your upset. Let's be honest...I think we all know a few people who love to ride their power trip and just be a jerk. But there's a clever way to go about this, no matter which way they might be acting.

When facing this email, as I reply, I take the time to say, "Oh my goodness, it looks like you did not see this (whatever) that I'd sent you." Or, "I know it's been a while since our phone call, and life gets crazy. From my notes, let me just refresh the conversation, and see if you remember things the same as I do." I also might say something like, "Let me start from the beginning." If it was something you already have in writing and they are disputing? "Hmm. Let me send you a screenshot. This is what I was going off of," and see how they respond.

Almost every time I use a phrase such as that. In doing so, it allows me to feel upset and write out my point, but be clear and non-accusatory. I think sometimes we all feel a little attacked in a message. By replying like this, it gives the other person an easy way out (Oh yes, I forgot. Sorry) and a justification for the upset they felt, but your kind and calm reply does not add fuel to their fire. Now remember what I said about scheduling your emails? This is an important thing to remember. If at all possible, and you are replying by email, then schedule that email. If it's something that needs a quick reply, maybe schedule it for an hour from now. Once sent, an email gets read and there are no backsies! Like a text message, read it one more time very carefully. Don't skip over any of the words the last time before you send it.

But what if you do get too emotional?

If you do start to cry, get upset, or some other emotional response bursts out and you just simply can't help it, try to relax. Take a few deep breaths. When this happens to me, I apologize. (I know, I know, supposed to be unapologetic, right?! But I do apologize for this, and here's why.) I say, "I apologize. This is very upsetting for me, and I'm still trying to process what happened." Oddly enough, just saying that phrase helps me to calm down. It's like I've given myself that compassion and understanding. I'm saying: "Self, this is hard. I see that. But you can do it."

Once I've said that, it's amazing how suddenly I can get myself under control somewhat. I've acknowledged my emotions, apologized for being difficult to understand for a moment, and moved forward. You can do it too. Just keep going.

Another thing I do is I practice. Just like you would before a play, I say all of my lines. The lines are everything I want to say. And I do it again. And again. I imagine myself in that doctor's office, that teacher meeting, whatever. And I repeatedly tell MY side, MY concerns, whatever it is that needs to be heard from ME. I get all my nerves out and get all of my thoughts aligned. I do this over and over. When I do, I find I'm able to talk later with so many less nerves. I seem to remember what it is I want to say. I feel confident in my word choices because I have practiced them. This practicing not only helps you feel more comfortable with what you want to say, it also helps you remember it.

Have you ever seen the movie *Finding Nemo*? My favorite character is Dory. Dory is a bit spacy, as she suffers from what she calls "short term remembery loss," but she's really smart. Not only does she repeat the things she wants to remember, she also has some pretty good advice. If you know Dory, you know her song...just keep swimming. Don't ever stop, just swim...swim. I have both a bracelet and a small sign with that quote. There are a lot of times in life you're going to have to just keep swimming. It's not going to be all clear and calm water. Sometimes it's going to be murky, or shark filled. But unless you want to stay stuck, staying in the exact same place, you've got to swim.

Communication and emotions are all part of that swim. They also play such a key role in getting the help that our children need to advocate for themselves. This communication—in the proper way—is something that not only builds up the support team but also provides documentation when something does go wrong and the ball gets dropped somewhere.

This proper documentation also allows you to go back and refer to things. Perhaps you check to see what way you had been doing something, so that if it wasn't working you could try something different. The more detailed you can become with your communication, the better it is.

Keep a folder on your laptop or a running list on Google Docs. Whatever it is, just make sure that you are keeping notes, scheduling your emails, and reading and rewriting. And of course, just keep swimming.

14

THE BINDER

When it comes to documentation, there's another piece that you might find useful, and it was actually suggested to me by another parent as something they found important to have. After the suggestion, I realized she was right!

A binder that can hold all of your papers together is quite valuable. Not only will there be things you'll have signed (IEP, IHP, 504 Plan, miscellaneous school forms) and want copies of, but there will also be papers from a medical provider that you might need to pull out at a moment's notice.

Having one central place for all of these papers to sit, be collected, and ready to pull out as needed is really important. You don't need anything fancy. You can do something as simple as make a three-ring binder with page protectors or dividers. There are also expandable file folders in binder form, with pocketed folders already in there. Whatever works best with your style of organizing is the important thing. If you won't use it, it's been a waste of time, effort, and money. Choose something where you'll be able to put your papers in easily, but then also find them again quickly when the time comes. Browsing any office supply store is a good start.

The benefit of having this binder is not only will you have all the documentation that you need in one place, you'll also be (and look!) prepared for any meetings with school staff or doctors. It's a bit harder for something to be denied or someone to argue with you when you've got that paper from three months ago you were given, or a print out of an email from six months prior. For myself, I know I'd be both in awe, and a little intimidated if someone showed up to a meeting with a three-inch binder packed and nearly organized. It would tell me that they knew what they were talking about, and I needed to pay attention. That's the goal, and a huge part of advocating, showing you are prepared and you know what you are talking about.

Additional items that might be helpful to add are a pen and plain paper, and a single sheet with contact information on it for each person in the binder. Be sure to store this in an easy to get to place, and do not forget where you've put it!

If you aren't quite where to start, Google can help you out! Just type in something like IEP binder or printable medical binder and see what pops up. There will be a lot of free printables and inspiration from other caregivers to get you started. Seeing the different ways that other people use these binders will help you to figure out what might work best for you. Remember, it doesn't have to be complicated or expensive. The purpose is simply to have all of your needed documentation and information in one place.

15

SIX STEPS FOR SUCCESSFUL ADVOCATING

You've learned what an advocate is, and tips to help your child learn to be one as well. Now, a brief guide with six steps for successful advocating. Use these tips as you move forward and need to advocate in medical, education, or family and friend settings. No one step is more important than the other. Each is like a piece of your advocating foundation.

Step 1: Prepare

This is where your documentation is going to come in handy. Whether it's on your phone, in a notebook, or on your computer, make sure you document. Phone calls, doctor or school visits, who, what, when, where, why. Your documentation is also going to help you if you become flustered, overwhelmed, or talked over. You can push that emotional response aside and stick to the facts with your notes.

Step 2: Know your stuff

How can you know if what is being suggested for your child is the best course of action unless you know something about the process and what it entails? That goes for everything. Medical plans, educational processes, everything. Beforehand, decide what you want the outcome to be. Brainstorm ways to get that outcome. What do you need to suggest that they might not have thought of?

Step 3: Take it seriously

If you want to be taken seriously, you need to be professional in everything. In how you dress, in how you talk, in each email you send. Don't show up to an important meeting in pajama bottoms and a stained sweatshirt. Familiarize yourself with the proper language regarding what you are there to discuss. No one expects you to be perfect or have a full grasp of everything, but show that you are competent and should be taken seriously.

Step 4: Be present

Make eye contact. Shake hands. Nod. Ask questions, and don't be too shy to voice opinions. This is your child's wellbeing at stake. Pay attention to what's said, even if you don't fully understand it. Don't be on your phone or let yourself get distracted or your attention wander.

Step 5: Practice positivity

Start off the meeting with a smile and a positive attitude. Don't think the worst coming in. You are feeling so stressed and defensive, but there's a good chance that those other people in the meeting are too! Foster an atmosphere of teamwork, and professional behavior.

Step 6: Be appreciative

No matter how the meeting ends, thank everyone for their time and for caring enough about your child to come together. No matter who is there, each person has their own life problems on top of work problems and you've no idea what type of day they've had. Being grateful and recognizing their efforts might even be just what you need to get the results you are looking for.

PART TWO

Medical

16

GETTING A DIAGNOSIS

Sometimes it can be hard to get help for something. Maybe it's getting a diagnosis for your child who struggles while reading. It could be no one knows what is causing those headaches or that pain. Medical or educational, there usually must be a diagnosis in order to move forward in getting the help and the plan that your child needs.

There are multiple places you can seek help. A good start is your child's doctor. However, often, that's easier said than done. While there are many great doctors who care, there are also those who are rushed, aren't sympathetic, aren't informed on something, or don't take you seriously. Chances are good, you've run into that yourself with your own care.

At times, you may have to do research on your own. Perhaps you are limited because of the area you live in, and may need to expand your search for a provider. Your insurance company, if you have one, can also provide a list of suggestions for in and out of network care. Do not forget though, that just like you don't know everything, doctors do not either. That's why second and third opinions or a fresh perspective might be just the thing that your child needs.

Recently, long covid has emerged. With it, it's brought a greater awareness of those who suffer chronically from long-term illnesses caused by viruses. One thing most every doctor can agree on when examining these patients is that no two patients present with symptoms the same way, and there's just not enough data to help figure out what is needed. Using post viral chronic illnesses as an example, some people experience fatigue, intense headaches, and limb weakness. Others, the symptoms might be of widespread inflammation, GI issues, and lack of appetite. Still, others might have lost the ability to walk and have nerve pain that doesn't ease.

I used this as an example because just as no one person presents the same way with a chronic illness, neither will multiple people present with the exact same symptoms for any medical or educational issue. There's a reason why a medication will list "possible side effects" and why IHPs, IEPs, and 504 Plans are personalized. Some will have or need one thing, some will not. Others will overlap in what they have.

Because of this, it's very possible that you will not be able to get the diagnosis your child needs with a one size fits all approach. Obtaining the diagnosis is often only the first step. Once you have it, you may need to repeat this process of finding doctors in order to actually get the help your child needs, as often multiple people will be involved in the care plan.

This next section is going to give you some suggestions on finding your provider, and what things you, as your child's advocate, need to be aware of.

17

TRUST YOUR INSTINCTS

We all tend to doubt ourselves. Why? Is it we feel like we don't know as much as others do? Sure, maybe we don't know everything...but we know a lot. And when it comes to our children, we know them better than anyone else does.

Think about a time in the past when you knew something was wrong with your child. Chances are, you were right. But what did others think? That you were imagining it? Overreacting? Crazy? The thing is, when it comes to our kids, no one knows better than us. No one will care for, love them like, advocate for, or tirelessly help, the way we will.

Because of this, your instincts aren't wrong. Tap into that inner gut feeling. Don't dismiss it. When you get that strange feeling when it comes to your child's medical or education care, listen to it. Research on your own. Come to your own conclusions. Now, I'm not saying ignore your doctor. But if you feel like something isn't right... trust that feeling, and seek additional guidance. Your child deserves that, and YOU deserve to be listened to.

Part of this ties back into the self-advocating. Remember those people who wished they'd just pressed harder for an answer? Or those people who were so glad they did? You are in their shoes right now, standing at that crossroad. Are you willing to take a chance and ignore that feeling in your stomach, staying the course because the doctor you saw knows best? Or are you going to start searching for answers, and get the help that your gut is saying you need?

It's time to trust yourself. You have that innate sense of concern, of a burning need to search for answers for a reason. Listen to yourself. Don't let others plant a seed of doubt into your mind. Within you is a strong advocate who knows something isn't quite right. Help them to figure it out, by trusting your instincts.

18

DOCTORS / MEDICAL SETTINGS

When my oldest was an infant, he had a pediatrician at a large practice, a good practice, but I always felt like we were ignored. My baby and I would wait for a scheduled appointment sometimes over an hour in the exam room waiting to be seen. One day at his two-year-old checkup, it had been almost ninety minutes we were left in the exam room, on top of over an hour in the waiting room. I flagged down a nurse, asked what was going on, and she shrugged. A while later, the doctor came in. He told me I should have more patience. I explained I'd been there for over two hours past my scheduled appointment, with a tired and hungry toddler. He just shrugged. Then, he opened my son's file, and said, "I see Conner is ready for his next round of vaccines."

"Conan," I answered. "His name is Conan."

Once again, the doctor shrugged. "Doesn't matter," he said. "Close enough."

Didn't matter? My son, his patient, didn't matter? *Close enough?* What else wouldn't matter with his care? What else would be "close enough"?

When we left, at the checkout I asked to be moved to a different doctor. I had it put in my son's chart he would never be treated by this doctor. If a doctor can't be bothered to say the name on the chart that's in front of them, how can you trust them to take care of your child? If they can't be bothered to treat a patient or the patient's parent with respect in a conversation, how can they have their best interests at heart?

Over the years, we've had good doctors and mediocre doctors. Oddly enough, and in part because of the rural area that we live in and the limited number of doctors available, I actually choose to keep both the mediocre doctors and the good ones. Each has a particular personality and a way of doing things that suits what I need for my child.

For example, we have two allergists. One is fantastic about answering the phones and writing epipen prescriptions, no questions asked when we need them. The other is an incredibly knowledgeable allergist who I feel comfortable can answer my questions in a non-judgmental way, yet it's nearly impossible to get hold of them. The staff almost never answers the phone and they are a satellite location, so they're only there a few days a week and still almost an hour's drive away.

Of course, it's ideal, and it's absolutely best if you can get one doctor for all of your child's medical needs, but the reality is that may not happen. It's important that you create a team of doctors. Build a team of medical support staff, so that no matter what comes up, you know you have someone who can help you. This could be a pediatrician, a preferred person at the urgent care clinic, and a particular specialist, including nurses or physician assistants or nurse practitioners, all of who work at a certain place your child or you feel comfortable with, and are willing and able to help you however you need without a feeling of judgment being placed. It's especially important to have a support team medically because these are also the people who will be talking to staff at your child's school if they have needs that should be given extra consideration.

While, of course, we would all like to think a school will believe absolutely everything we say, and do it exactly the way we want, (I go into this more depth into the school section) the reality is each school and each school district will have its own way things are handled, including what information is given or requested to those caring for your child.

You'll need to give your consent on this, and it may be optional, but I have found by giving my consent and making the school nurse a part of my son's support team, the school does not feel like I'm trying to hide anything or over-exaggerate it. Additionally, the nurse feels partially responsible for my child's wellbeing in school. It's not that you are signing away complete control—quite the opposite. You have the right to tell your child's doctor what you want the school to or not to know. Meaning, if you think your child should have a special accommodation the doctor has not thought of, then see if they will tell the school your child needs that particular accommodation. Often when this information comes from a medical practitioner, the school is much more likely to oblige.

But what to do if you don't have this medical support team for your child? Times may arise when you don't. Perhaps your child is newly diagnosed or needs to be diagnosed with something. Maybe you've just moved and you haven't been able to get a referral or know anyone who can suggest a good doctor. Sometimes that unknowing adds so much stress!

How can you reduce that worry so you can focus on what your child needs? The answer to that question is another question: What are some questions that you might want to ask in order to get to know this doctor or find the right person to help your child? I have a list for you at the end of this section, but first let me explain a little why I suggest you always have a list of questions when going in to see a doctor or calling one.

Have you ever left an appointment and thought to yourself: "Oh rats! I wish I had asked that question!" Maybe the doctor seemed in a hurry and you felt like such a bother, so you decided the question wasn't that important after all...even if it was.

This happens to me sometimes! However, when I have that list of questions I've prepared ahead of time, I'm able to decide in the moment yes this is important and I need an answer, or no I can figure this out on my own I don't really need to take up any more time, and I've been waiting long enough I'm ready to go.

Too often doctors are told how long they can spend with a patient, and how many patients an hour they must see. This intense workload, and the time restrictions placed upon them, can cause you to feel like your visit was rushed. This is why preparing a bit about what you want to talk about can be very valuable.

When it comes to questions, if your child is with you, do they also have questions? As a parent or caregiver, it is always your decision as to how much you want to involve or not involve your child in their medical care. I do believe that if a child can be involved in their care, they should be. Using age-appropriate terminology and words not meant to alarm but to empower your child can really make it much easier for them to learn to become their own self-advocate.

Armed with my list, always, and never forgotten, is one question I ask my child. "Kiddo, what kind of questions do you have?" Sometimes that catches the doctor off guard, but other times it doesn't. Regardless, they always stop and look at my child and say, "Yes, what questions do you have?" So even if those questions are a little silly or if those questions are amazingly insightful, the doctor is there to listen to them and answer. Recently, I was thrilled after a recent doctor's visit when the doctor posed each of his questions to my youngest son, before talking to me. I'm seeing this more and more, as the doctors realize my child is his own advocate.

My children have asked everything from, for example, "Will you take all my blood out and then I won't have any?" to "What if that swab goes up too far and you push out my eyeball?" to the basic, "Will this hurt?" I'm proud when they speak up, instead of sitting there with those worries that might grow to be bigger than they can manage. How big some of those fears are that I never knew! And once knowing, I was able to help ease them. Additionally, I've never once had a doctor, even one who might have used a condescending tone with me, speak that way to my child even on what could be considered a silly question. The question is always answered, my child always learns, and then they respect that information because it came from a medical professional.

By giving my children the freedom to ask these questions, and encouraging them to self-advocate, I've watched as they do, in many situations. In fearful moments at the doctor's office, they ask for a moment to take a few breaths, or to be told step by step what's going to happen before something's done. How brave and incredible that is, and how much I wish I'd learned to do that myself sooner! In a place that's outside of your comfort zone, and what medical practice isn't, it feels empowering to have that small thing you are in control of. Sometimes it makes all the difference to you or your child, and the quality of their care.

Here are a few of the questions that I typically like to ask when meeting a new provider. You can use these as a starting point to make your own list. You can even create a master list, one that can be printed off before a new appointment. If you realize when you get to the appointment that you don't have a list, quickly create one on a scrap of paper or your phone. Google Docs can be used on your computer or through an app, and is very useful to keep a master list on because of how easily you can access it almost anywhere.

- Have you treated children with a diagnosis similar to my child's?

-

How often do you think we need to be seen for checkups?

- If there's an emergency, how should I get hold of you?

- Do you have emergency hours if I need to bring my child in, or should they go somewhere else?

- How soon do I get a call back if I call the nurse line?

- Where are some places I can research this diagnosis?

- What advice do you have for me to handle my child's needs?

- What kind of emotional or mental health concerns should I be looking for regarding this diagnosis?

- Is there anything you think I should know that you haven't told me?

I particularly like that last question because it makes the doctor pause, think back over what they've said, and if something had been fluttering at the edge of their minds, that's the time that they usually mention it. Sometimes you find out something very interesting or are given another fragment of help in this journey that you are now on.

A last word—don't be afraid to ask the doctor to repeat something. How often do we not do that? And then we wish, so very much, a short while later, we could remember what was said, or had understood it better. Isn't it silly to think that just a few seconds to ask and then listen carefully could prevent hours of wondering or online searching, yet we rarely do it?

19

HOSPITALS

When your child needs to visit a hospital, it's a whirlwind, especially if you are at the emergency room. There seems to be an endless stream of people coming in and out (except for when you want one!) and rarely are they the same faces.

On a recent ER trip with one son, within three hours, we'd had seven people come in the room. None of them the same person twice. That can lead to problems, especially if your child has a special need. Too often we think, "Ah! The hospital. They know what to do. I, the caregiver, can relax on my phone and let them take care of my kid. I don't want to get in their way!" So, we sit back, we watch, and we let them do their thing because they know best...right?

Wait a second! How is that an advocate behavior? Was I trying to trick you? I was! Good catch. Guess what? You are at a hospital, full of helpful folks, yes...but also tired, overworked, busy people. They might not remember that your kid needs this or can't have that. And not all hospitals have protocols in place to prevent those kinds of mistakes. You may also find that the level of care varies between who you see and where you are.

Two examples:

That recent ER trip, my youngest was wearing an allergy alert bracelet put on by the hospital. No one checked it. As they were preparing an IV for him and I asked what was in it, they looked at me like I had two heads. I explained the allergy, and asked again, what was in the IV. A few hours later, at 11 pm, someone decided my child needed to eat something. The nurse told me that as she walked in, and her hand was stretched out. Of course, my young son did what anyone of any age would do, when someone was holding something out. He reached for it.

Out of the corner of my eye, I saw she had brought in an open container of peanut butter, that he was severely allergic to, nearly putting it into his hand. Instinctively, I moved to intercept. She stared at me, and simply said "oops" as I said he was allergic, pointed to the allergy bracelet, and asked why it was necessary he eat something.

If I had been distracted, if I had let myself doze, confident he was in good care, and I was running on so little sleep the last few weeks, I might have missed what she held. After all, I thought the person was coming in to check vitals again. I wasn't expecting her to hand it to him, saying, "Here, eat this." I had to be aware of all possible complications, (allergens lurking in food or medicine) and be prepared for the staff not to notice.

The second example: My oldest went to the ER. It was, unfortunately, a situation he'd been in before, so I knew what he needed. However, I wasn't there, and when my son refused an IV with medicines, no one thought twice that it was a need, not a want. They were not as familiar with his medical need as I was. I was texting frantically, trying to explain to him WHY that was needed, and WHY certain other steps needed to be taken, and the absolute importance of those things, to get him to get the staff to give those things.

Because he was a little older, the doctor let my son influence the decision for the method of the medicine. He was still slightly worked up after using the epipen, feeling nervous and not his best, and when he refused, the doctor respected that decision. My son explained he felt better, and knew he'd get the medicines, they just seemed busy and he didn't want to take up anyone's time. As a result, while eventually he got the medicine he needed, it was in a pill form, not the IV form which would have been delivered to his body quicker.

In any medical setting, you have to be able to advocate. It might be you need to advocate for care or for a safe setting. You might even need to advocate to get testing done. Do not let that feeling of being in the way, being a bother, or fear of speaking up prevent you from finding the answers and getting the help that is needed. It can happen that you get overlooked, it can happen that things are busy, and if you don't ask you won't get what you need.

Advocate. It is your right, and it is your job. Don't let anything stop you. While you can expect a level of care when visiting a hospital, if there is a special concern or need, remember that it might not be taken as seriously as it should be. It might not even be known unless you make it known. It is your right to ask questions and get what is needed.

Don't let yourself feel rushed. If you need something repeated, ask for it to be repeated or explained in another way. Voice your concerns and questions, and do your best to get answers in person. It's much harder to get hold of someone later, when you are trying to get specific answers about a test result or a concern you have.

20

GETTING MEDICAL STAFF TO ADVOCATE FOR / WITH YOU

Of course, you understand the absolute importance of advocating. But do you ever feel like your voice alone isn't quite enough? In some situations, it might not be. This is why it's so important to have that medical team for your child that you can rely on.

Be it a medical or an educational challenge your child has, it's important they have a doctor willing to speak up for them to others. It's also incredibly important that you have a medical professional who is passionate about helping your child. Sometimes it's as simple as a doctor or nurse telling the insurance company that a therapy or medicine *is* needed and *should* be covered when the insurance company denies it. Other times, it might be helping you with a situation neither of you are familiar with. Doctors help other doctors. You might get into a specialist sooner, get a referral sooner, or even have a doctor willing to phone or text a colleague to get you help. Remember my story about my one child in the ER late at night? Let me back up just a little.

After recovering from a virus, my son suddenly had his fever return at the two-week mark. I took him in to see one of the doctors who often cared for him at a multi-physician practice. This doctor assured me it was just another virus, and he'd be fine in a few days. Except...he wasn't.

The fever continued for another week. When I phoned, I was told don't make an appointment. He was fine and I was overreacting. But that didn't feel right to me. I took him into the after-hours clinic offered by the practice on weekends. The second doctor, one we've also seen many times, was concerned when she heard the story. Bloodwork was ordered. My son and I waited quietly to be seen by the doctor. We could hear the first doctor through the wall. "It's not a big deal. I told them it's JUST a virus. That's it. They are over-exaggerating the importance."

When the doctor came in, the test results showed my son had seriously elevated blood platelet issues, and inflammation markers throughout his body in several organs. The plan was to watch him at home, bring him back in a few days and retest, hoping it was just a stubborn virus. However, at 7pm that night, the doctor called. "I don't feel right about this," the doctor said. "And I know it's a long drive for you to go to the children's hospital, but I've been talking to the doctors there, and they think he needs to be seen. Tonight." The doctor began to apologize, and I interrupted, saying, "Don't ever apologize for doing what you think is right when it comes to taking care of my child."

Fast forward a bit. The ER wouldn't admit my son because he didn't meet their criteria, though they admitted, if he did, they could treat him because they agreed something wasn't right. Over the next week, his fever continued. And he got weak. Over three weeks of fever at this point. Then he stopped eating and stopped drinking. He was losing weight dramatically. We saw this second doctor, and a third at the practice. Bloodwork was done repeatedly. There was no improvement. Then, this second doctor called me one evening. "I told them testing isn't good enough. They all agree what he has, (a lower spectrum of a serious post viral inflammation syndrome striking children in 2021 / 2022) and I told them he's wasting away. They still won't admit him. So I called, and I spoke to multiple people and I told them they had to give us a plan."

That doctor advocated for my child in a way I couldn't. Though that doctor has left the practice, I will be forever grateful to her. That doctor knew who to call, what to say, who to beg advice from. This was so new, so unusual, not a single doctor at my son's pediatrician's office knew what to do or how to treat it. Thankfully, they admitted that was the case, and sought help. While the specialists at the hospital admitted they also knew very little, they said children like my son were pouring in, and they were making educated guesses, trying things until they found something that would help.

He was started on a medicine. Unfortunately, it didn't do well for him. He was vomiting it up, and his mouth was filled with sores. At this point, he was severely dehydrated, and his tiny body was losing several pounds a week. He was exhausted, weak, and we were desperate. He still didn't meet criteria for admission. Doctors two and three now, increased the phone calls to the specialists at the children's hospital.

We stopped the medicine, switched to a new one, as advocated by the third doctor, and within days, I had glimpses of my happy, cheerful child again. He was eating a little more, drinking more, and two weeks later, had gained a pound. At the time of writing this, we aren't out of the woods yet. It's been nearly a year of ups and downs and scary things we don't have answers or help for. Every day we watch carefully to see how much he eats and drinks, how he acts to make sure he's not regressing or something else is happening. However, I do know, without a doubt, if I had not had these two doctors advocating for him, reaching the channels of help I could not, my son would be in much worse shape. The advocating has not stopped there.

As we've been to multiple specialists and been told "I don't know how to help you" I've turned to other parents with similar experiences, and learned things to take to my son's doctors to see if those would help him. Sometimes they do, sometimes they don't. But I don't stop trying, and I don't stop advocating.

When something feels wrong, it is wrong. It doesn't matter if it's a doctor who dismisses you, or that feeling inside. If it doesn't feel right to you, then explore that more. It's a sign you need to change something. However, there's a right way and a wrong way to push for that change.

It can be easy to get frustrated with the level of care your child gets. When you are tired, scared, or upset it is easy to get angry. It's not okay to act out like that, though. Angry just pushes the help you need away. It was hard hearing that my child could be helped if he could be admitted, but he didn't meet the criteria. I felt frustrated. Helpless. Exhausted from searching every avenue for his care. To this day, I wonder if he'd just gotten the help he needed right then, would he still have struggled so? In those early moments, knowing that I had two doctors also there, taking my phone calls, filling me in on what was going on, trying to find their own answers, that was incredibly valuable.

Part of advocating is finding those who will be on your child's side. Those who will advocate along with you. Those who are passionate, relentless, and unwavering in their care. Such people are out there. They do exist. Work to find them, and when you do, make sure to thank them for helping you, for helping your child. They need to know how very valuable they are to you. This one doctor spoke with medical staff well after working hours. This doctor has their own family and children, but was worried about mine.

As you work with individuals in the healthcare environment, remember that part of building a team is to work with them. Be polite. Watch as they make notes. Don't be afraid to ask them to make sure something is jotted down. If they want to send your child to a specialist, ask who they prefer. Ask if they have heard good things. Taking a little time to ask their honest opinion can sometimes provide you with the absolute best match for your child, not just a doctor, therapist, or other care provider who can do whatever thing needed to be done or checked on. You are looking for a team member, not a box to be checked off. By doing this, you will find a natural advocate for your child.

If you ever feel like you aren't getting the care your child needs, if you aren't being taken seriously, it's time to look for another doctor, and to keep looking until you find one.

There is someone out there who can help your child. You just have to find them.

You know what's best for your child. You have that instinct given to you. When something doesn't feel right, when you can't get the answers you know are out there, keep going. Find that person to help you. They do exist, you just need to keep looking. Don't stop until you find them.

21

INSURANCE ADVOCATING

When it comes to medical needs, there is one more place that you often need to advocate, and that is with your insurance company if you have one. Don't be afraid to call. Often they are very kind and helpful and will give you all the information that you need to know, such as doctors in or out of network, if you need a referral, and what your coverage is. Since many of us don't know each and every detail of our insurance policies inside and out, and insurance companies know this, they are used to these kinds of calls, and will tell you what you need to know.

While there will be someone at the medical provider's office to advocate for you for coverage, don't be afraid to dispute charges yourself, or question denial of services. While your medical provider might be able to get through the red tape a little quicker, that doesn't mean you shouldn't try as well. Getting something covered is important.

Ask what options are available to help your child that your child's doctor might not have even considered. One such thing would be a service dog. Not just for those with vision impairment, service dogs also help those with seizures or other complex medical conditions, such as diabetes, PTSD, food allergies, and autism.

While service dogs aren't paid for by your insurance company, you can, with approval, use Flexible Spending Account funds for them. This might be a time you need to advocate to have those funds approved.

There may also be other medical equipment needs your child has that aren't covered by insurance. Before you give up and assume the out of cost for that, check with your doctor first. Sometimes they can advocate for the items to be considered medically necessary and covered, other times your insurance will agree to let you use those Flexible Spending Account funds or Health Savings Account funds on them.

Be sure to keep track of your medical receipts, not just to be sure you aren't overcharged, but also to make sure it's correctly applied to any deductible you have with your insurance company. Depending on the amount spent, these receipts also might be valuable for your end of the year tax deductions.

PART THREE

Education

22

School

A few years ago, during the early part of the coronavirus pandemic when children moved to virtual education, my oldest son started failing science and math. I was surprised, but believed him when he said he was doing the work. In the back of my mind, I did wonder, *but is he turning it in?* It happens, right? Kids do the work, but don't always turn it in on time or at all. We began tracking everything he did and when he did it. There were emails to the teacher, meetings, and the teacher continued to say she wasn't getting his work.

I grew suspicious. Each day I watched him turn in his work. She still didn't get it. I taught him to screenshot the assignment submissions and the assignments. We had proof the assignments were submitted. Still, he was failing. There were constant emails at this point, daily phone calls. We were told he wasn't doing submissions right. Screenshots didn't matter and they didn't count toward the grade. I was spending hours each week on the phone and emailing the school administration and the teacher insisting this wasn't right.

Then came the day my son clicked on an assignment to prove to me it was done, and it said it was in the owner's trash. The teacher's trash. We took a screenshot, and I left a voicemail with the school. A short time later...it wasn't there in her trash anymore. It was completely gone. If it had not been for that perfect timing, it would have looked like again, an assignment he completed was gone.

I'm going to back up just a little. Over the course of this year, I watched my brilliant, computer whiz kid who can type faster than me, who has taught himself to program, and was in a cyber security program, someone who knows how to use a computer and use it well, lose all of his self-esteem. He started to panic before classes. He turned the opposite of how he had been, only enjoying his classes with the other teachers, never this one.

My child wasn't alone in this. Many children in this class gave up. Others took the failing grades. None of them wanted to get their parents involved. Some said because they thought their parents wouldn't care, others because they were scared their situation would get worse. Things getting worse was my son's concern, and he didn't want me to get involved at first.

However, I didn't let this go. The very day we saw his work in the trash, I was on the phone. A short time later, the school system tech support was involved. Sure enough, they tracked his assignments and discovered they had been trashed by the teacher. My son was pulled from her class immediately, and slowly got his confidence in himself back.

But what happened to the teacher, you might wonder? She stayed on. Other children in her class have told my son how shaky they still get passing her classroom door. How they hate to walk anywhere near the classroom. But no one else stood up for their child. I don't even know if these other parents understood the severity of the psychological abuse these children were getting.

If you look in the news, you'll hear similar stories. Chances are you could find several recent events without even scrolling far. This morning I woke up to several on my feed that horrified me.

You'll also hear about children feeling uncomfortable because they walk down their school hallway and someone touches them inappropriately. I know many children in elementary, middle, and high school that has happened to. But nothing is done. Sometimes their parents don't want to say anything. Sometimes it's the child who doesn't want to.

What about bullying? Such an incredibly common act, where it's usually only after a serious incident or it lands in the news something is done. There are those bullied by both students and teachers, but no one stops it. Maybe the school system denies it, because they take a firm stance and such a thing couldn't happen! Then there could also be the fact there is an incredible amount of pressure to keep children in schools, no matter what. Kids don't like to report things, because they are often scared of retaliation or a situation being ignored. They figure, why bother?

Regardless of the situation, one thing is sure. *Advocacy for your child is important in many situations.* Their education, their safety, their confidence.

Let's talk about education first.

Not all children are those called traditional learners. Interestingly enough, the vast majority of those considered not to be traditional learners are male. In a setting like education, where the majority of the field is female dominated, that can bring about difficulties for advocating a male student's needs. If you want to dig deeper into this topic, there is quite a bit of research available online. But let's keep going. What is this traditional learner?

A traditional learner is defined as one in a classroom where the teacher is leading discussions and for the student, learning, and sitting, and listening for that entire school day is an important trait. Some children can sit well, and can listen and learn from something being drawn on the board at the front of the room, or from paper packets to complete being passed out in each class. Others cannot. These children need the freedom to move around, experience deep dives into information instead of surface facts, like to be hands-on or are visual learners, or may excel at project-based assignments where tests make them freeze.

There are several personality types for children, and I believe they play a huge role in the style of education that works best for them. Education isn't, and shouldn't be, a one size fits all approach, yet how often is it? Some children are more serious, others sensitive. Some need to be active and are outgoing, while others prefer to sit quietly and work alone. It can be hard at times in a school setting to make sure each child and their unique learning style and needs are met. When you add to that classroom that there are children who have medical needs and learning challenges, phew...that's a lot for a teacher or school or parent to figure out so the child is learning successfully and thriving! Most schools are simply just not prepared to take on those challenges and the multiple learning styles that exist.

The Supreme Court established FAPE (Free and Appropriate Education) as part of the 1973 Rehabilitation Act and IDEA (Individuals with Disabilities Education Act). It states that schools need to provide this free and appropriate education to all students. However, schools only need to show that students are making adequate progress. FAPE isn't limitless in its right to have. For example, this free and appropriate education doesn't require schools to provide the best services possible for students. It also doesn't require that each student's potential be maximized.

Additionally, it doesn't mean that schools have to offer a specific educational program, no matter how good it is, or even provide a specific class setting that a parent wants their child to have. When it comes to sports or extracurriculars, it also doesn't guarantee a spot in that activity or any special treatment. FAPE only requires schools to provide services that are considered to be reasonably calculated to help the student make progress.

Because of this, as upsetting as it is, it's unrealistic to expect schools to tailor every aspect of the education world to a single student. They just have to do the minimum to ensure they can learn. This is why advocating, and having the proper plan set up for your child (IEP, IHP, or 504 Plan) is incredibly critical.

There is a lot to take into consideration when it's time for school and special medical needs. In between classroom parties and learning activities, as well as the special classes your child might have such as music or physical education, there's always some way that they'll need to be accommodated.

When you add in off-campus events like field trips or maybe extra special events such as field day or PTO or PTA activities, holidays, substitute teachers, afterschool programs, and others who might come into contact with your child to teach or simply be around, there's definitely a lot that you'll need to think about and let the school staff know. Many times, even if your child has an IEP, IHP, or 504 Plan, not all adults will know this. Even if they are aware, they might not have a copy of that information available to them to see your child is included in the way they (and you) have been promised.

Something else to remember is that not every staff member is going to think as far ahead as you do as a parent. It could be a busy moment and this special need slipped their mind. For example, a teacher may be planning out their lessons two weeks in advance and simply forget what they are doing until the day of. Perhaps it involves some sort of movements in PE class your child is unable to do. Maybe there is some sort of reading activity or a food activity and your child can't fully participate because they have difficulty reading or the food isn't one that is safe for them. There are children with various medical conditions who can't or shouldn't eat something. They should still be thought of when food is included in a lesson or an activity. For the child who cannot read easily or has limited speech, there needs to be some way for them to easily take part in Reader's Theatres or school plays without making them feel different or embarrassed they are participating in a different way.

Not all children can physically do certain things, but they still need to be a part of the lessons taught. That is their legal right as a public school attendee. It's important that your child's teacher always has in the forefront of their mind inclusion for your child, and you can help create that by always being visible. It's also important that the school staff knows what your child needs, and helps provide it.

Take note of any educational activity that a child cannot complete or participate in due to their limitations. They should not be assessed or graded on that assignment if they were not able to participate. While most teachers are adept at teaching a concept in multiple ways, if your child is not able to join their peers, it could lead to a decline in their academic performance and affect them later on a topic they needed to know.

One teacher shared with me a story, about early in their teaching career several science teachers viewed doing labs as a reward, and so would not let some students participate due to a behavioral issue. When later, doing science labs became a mandatory form of instruction, those students were left behind because they did not have the knowledge of past participation, including things that others took for granted they knew, such as safe ways to handle the chemicals and supplies, and how to protect themselves.

Because in a school setting, often the advocating needs to be done ahead of time, we're going to talk a little bit more about this and break it down step by step, situation by situation, so that you can be prepared to discuss with your child's school any accommodations made for them in order to get the same school experience as their peers, which is their right.

23

START TO BUILD A FOUNDATION

It's important to build a foundation of support at your child's school. Many people are not even aware of the fact they aren't inclusive to a child until it's pointed out or noticed. This is where being visible is so important. Make yourself available. Answer emails or texts quickly. Just as you built your medical team, now you build the education team.

Start being a larger part of the school atmosphere by being a classroom parent or joining the PTO/PTA and attending meetings! Let your child's teacher know you are not only available for questions, but you can help volunteer and donate for various classroom things, if needed. Let the school staff know that as well. Volunteer, make yourself be seen, and be smiling and positive.

Just being there can have a positive impact on the relationship you have with the school staff and the relationship they have with your child. Whether it's offering once a week to come in and make copies for an hour to help the teachers or shelve books to help the librarian, there's always so much that can be done or offered to help the school staff, but also become a familiar face. Being that familiar face is the goal.

Though you have a lot on your plate, and your child's inclusion might be forefront in your mind, work toward the inclusiveness of ALL. What I mean is, if your school is planning a school wide fundraiser with a bounce house and ice cream as a reward, ask if they'd consider ice pops, so those with special dietary needs could join in. And see if some of them could be sugar or dye free for those who need it. If there's someone who would have trouble getting in a bounce house, could they have a special time with just them and a friend or staff member to play together for a little?

Before long, this mindset of how can I include others becomes contagious. While others might not want to carry that banner, it's possible they will ask you to. And then when other parents find out there's an advocate for THEM on the PTO/PTA, they get excited. They want to help and be involved because inclusiveness is no longer something that seems unattainable.

That change *does* happen, I promise. Recently, after nine years of serving our school PTO in some way or another, we had to stop and leave the school because of health concerns. I couldn't help it...after that first meeting of no longer being part of the PTO, I read the meeting notes posted online. Though I didn't attend, I was curious. There was a large event coming up. Would anyone remember those who might need to be thought of? To my absolute surprise, several of the things I was always the voice of for inclusion, someone else had brought up. I got all teary. I felt really proud too, because the people who had brought it up were not people who usually would. They were not people who usually ever wanted to be seen. But they felt that need to step up and advocate for others, and hopefully they will continue to advocate until their time is up, and become an example so that when they leave, others carry on with advocating for the students in the school during their time.

Many times, it's not that others don't care. It's that they don't think about it. They don't experience the same challenges and reality that you do, so it's never even occurred to them that things are different or that there could be a different way. What's always worked for them has always worked well for them, so they just can't imagine how hard it is for another family who lives with challenges daily to participate in something. They don't have that personal experience and are going to be relying on you to speak up.

It is so important that you be seen as someone working toward a change, not someone who is complaining. While yes, the squeaky wheel gets the grease, it also gets an annoyed look, and it's often the shopping cart at the grocery store left behind while you look for a team player, that cart with all four wheels working properly so you can just get your job done and move on to the next thing!

It's not only fun and rewarding to volunteer, but it's so desperately needed. Often, we all think that there is an army in the background making things happen, but usually there's not. In reality, it's just a few tired and overworked individuals who want to make things better for everyone and would welcome any help. I see this repeatedly in places I volunteer at. When I've tried to get others to help, they hide and ignore phone calls or emails. When an event has to be canceled because there was no help to run it, there are complaints. Helping is part of becoming visible. Being visible and volunteering allows those changes that you desire for your child to take place.

But what if something unspeakable happens, and exclusion is done deliberately? It is never okay for any adult to make fun of your child for a disability or medical condition. If that ever happens in a school setting from a staff member, a substitute, a volunteer, or anyone else connected to the school, immediately report it to the school administration. That is not an acceptable thing to happen and your child should not be treated poorly because of something they have no control over. In many cases, it might even be a violation of the Americans with Disabilities Act.

Seeking accommodations or advocating for your child isn't because you want special treatment. It's because you want them to have the same experiences (if at all possible) that other students get to enjoy. If your child goes to a public school, it is your tax dollars paying for this. If your child goes to a private school, you are paying tuition. It's only right that your child has a similar experience as their peers.

As you approach school staff with your child's needs, remember to go with an attitude of working together to help your child. Keep your concerns, questions, and responses based fully on your child's inclusion and the accommodations your child needs to empower them to get the education and school experience they deserve.

Now, let's discuss some of the individuals and situations you might need to use your newly acquired advocating skills on.

24

SUBSTITUTE TEACHER

I'm putting a substitute teacher ahead of the classroom teacher because a substitute teacher is a unique concern. They don't know your child's medical needs and quite often they're not even told about them because of HIPAA (Health Insurance Portability and Accountability Act) violation possibilities or because no one remembered to let them know. Not every substitution of a teacher is planned. Many are last minute and things fall through the cracks. That includes people, like your child. While every school district is going to be handling this differently, there needs to be some sort of plan in place with your school, the school nurse, your child's teachers, and any other adults they may come into contact with, like lunchroom staff, so that if there is a substitute, the child can be taken care of in the best way possible.

So, what might that look like? Of course, you need to work with your child's school or teacher in order to find the best solution that works for everyone, but some suggestions might be to have your child go into another teacher's classroom for the day. Request a teacher that they're already familiar with because perhaps they have a class or two each day with them. Another suggestion is to have a special folder with your child's picture on the front, along with their name and their medical information included in the substitute teacher folder. There can be a list of contact phone numbers as well as step-by-step instructions on what to do and where the buzzer is located at to call the front office or how they can get hold of the school nurse quickly. Other things that would need to be included on there may be the child's medical condition, but also any sort of medications they needed, things to look for in case of a potential problem, and perhaps even if they are feeling unwell to have a classmate walk them up to the front, if not calling for the nurse to come to the room.

If this substitute teacher is not the main classroom teacher but one for PE, Music, Art, or anything else, then talk with your child's teacher about what their standard way of handling this is, so your child can fully take part in whatever the class will do that day. It's quite possible they've never made arrangements for that situation, but upon looking back, they can remember a time where something did happen, and it wasn't inclusive for a child.

With a substitute teacher, it's best not to take any chances and remind the school of that. If your child has a medical need where they must get medications at particular times, the substitute teacher should be aware of that, and not punish the child for requesting to see the school nurse. If they should not eat anything that has not been approved by a parent, that information needs to be in there as well, so that the substitute does not pass out a treat as a reward or dole out a birthday treat another child has brought in without knowing your child cannot eat it.

So often, children think that the adults in the room know their needs and will remember to see they get that help. And that is not always the case. This is also another point where your child will need to learn to self-advocate. Warn them that if there is an unfamiliar person in the room that day and that person seems to be in charge of the class, they need to let the adult know that they have special accommodations provided by the school, in case something is wrong so that they can quickly get help for the child.

If the accommodation needed for your child is one that is physical or for a learning disability, the substitute being aware is incredibly important! A sub for PE might not be aware a child can't catch a ball. One for Art might not understand a child's difficulty in gripping a regular sized paintbrush or know where the child's special one is located in the regular teacher's cabinet. They also might not know if a child is colorblind and needs additional help in getting their supplies for a project. If this was an unplanned absence, it's possible the teacher didn't leave a note about this for the sub or even thought about it.

The same thing is true for a child who might need to leave at a particular time for education services, or have a special accommodation made for schoolwork. If a child is allowed to have a test read to them and the substitute teacher doesn't know that the child may visit the special education classroom for extra help, it could be marked as a failing grade.

A substitute teacher can't know something unless they are told, which is why a caregiver must advocate for their child ahead of any potential absences of the classroom teacher.

25

CLASSROOM SETTINGS

In our local school district, students have what are called "specials" each day. I'm sure they're called something different in other places, but these are the classes that are not typically classroom classes. Things like art, music, physical education, library, guidance, etc. Some children have off-campus Bible study class. While each of these teachers should be aware of any needs or accommodations a child has, it's important to make sure that you personally reach out to the teacher and touch bases with him or her, ideally before the child enters the classroom. The earlier you can talk to the teacher, the easier it is for them to make an accommodation, especially if it requires modifying a lesson. Most teachers use the same lesson plan year after year, so they might be on autopilot when prepping the lessons. The thought that this particular lesson might not work for everyone may not cross their mind.

For example, in a physical education class, a child who is unable to move a certain way should still be allowed to participate with their classmates and enjoy moving around. Perhaps the coach can modify her lesson so that each time all the children are doing the same thing, and no one knows that it's because one child cannot to something else. However, if your child has a heart condition and should not get their heart rate up over a certain beat per minute, the coach needs to be keeping a close eye on your child to make sure that they are not getting overexerted. Your child also needs to know when they are starting to get their heart rate a little too high, so that they can let the coach know they need to slow down or stop. Be sure that there are no consequences for your child's genuine need to not participate in something, and remind your child this is a serious thing, not something to take advantage of unnecessarily.

Sometimes, you know the solution but the teacher does not, because this is the first time they've needed to make this particular sort of accommodation. In an art class, a child who is not able to hold crayons or markers very easily might find a solution would be to have a thicker crayon or marker that's available for their use. Here, the mobility and fine motor skill need is accommodated in a way where your child feels included and gets to enjoy an educational setting. However, while you might have known this because your child uses these larger crayons at home, the art teacher might not have thought of it because they've always done things one particular way, and never needed to accommodate for this particular thing before. This is why it's so important to meet and speak with the teachers before your child is in their classroom.

One thing that many do not realize is most teachers do not get any special training for medical situations. The same goes for a substitute teacher. In many states, for example Virginia, a teacher only needs to be *exposed* to how to give CPR, not actually be trained in it. Teachers may be given information packets or assigned videos to watch, but that does not take the place of in-depth training. If your child has a medical need, it's important the teacher be aware and feel comfortable assisting as the adult in the room if there is a problem, and no one else is able to help.

For all needs, make sure that the teacher knows the school nurse is aware of your child's situation, and they may also have creative solutions for inclusion and accommodation. If your child needs extra help to get from point A to point B or if they need assistance in the classroom because of a learning disability, it's very important that they get that help and it should be given automatically if your child has a IHP, IEP, or 504 Plan. All teachers should make it a point to ensure all students feel included and welcome in the classroom.

Remember, most people do not think about things other than what they've previously experienced. The majority of people are happy to make exceptions and provide help if it can reasonably be done. They just are not aware of the need unless it is brought to them. It could be that your child's teacher has never had a student with a need like yours has. This is a great time to go in and explain to them how your child is still a normal child who enjoys doing normal child things. They just might need a little bit of help in this situation or that situation. As a caregiver, it's likely that you know many ways to handle a situation that an educator may not be aware of. Make a list, then go in and talk with them about possible scenarios that may arise, and how they can be handled in a way that includes your child but doesn't cause disruption to the classroom setting.

For example, if your child has a difficult time using a zippered pencil box but the school supply list says it has to be zippered and not a hard plastic one, then explain that your child needs the plastic case. For the child who has difficulty seeing well, even with glasses, you need to let the teacher know that throughout the school year, your child needs to sit near the front of the classroom, even if the teacher likes to have students switch seats frequently. If your child has a food allergy, perhaps there needs to be some sort of accommodation made, not just in the classroom but in the lunchroom as well.

No matter the situation, no matter the need, there is a way to accommodate and give inclusiveness, but also to prevent the child from being singled out and made to feel embarrassed.

26

CLASSROOM PARTIES OR HOLIDAY CELEBRATIONS

I don't know about you, but it definitely seems like there are a lot more classroom parties nowadays than there used to be when I was in school! It seems like everything is an excuse to have a party, and while that can be fun for some, for other kids these constant celebrations can make them feel left out.

Does your family not celebrate particular holidays because of your religious beliefs? Then what will your child be doing during that classroom celebration? Some teachers will completely change classroom traditions to make Halloween events fall themed, or eliminate holiday events. Others will simply send the child down to the library or the front office to sit for an hour. The same might go for Family Life Education, if your child is opted out. They have to go somewhere and do something during the school hour...so what will that be?

It's important that your child be included in some way. If other children are having a party, it wouldn't be right to send yours to the hallway with a book or worksheets. Ask before these events are even on the radar. Be prepared to both ask questions and provide possible solutions if the teacher has none or is unsure what to do in those instances.

For those with dietary restrictions such as a food allergy or diabetes, a party or food in a classroom lesson is actually a parent's worst nightmare. You're very worried about what might be brought in, especially with lookalike foods, if you are an allergy family. A lookalike food is something that looks identical to a national brand food, but is a different brand than your child is familiar with. For example, if you were to go to the store and find Chips Ahoy cookies, the kind in the blue package, flip it over and read the label. Then go to three different stores and compare that label on the Chips Ahoy brand to the store brand version. You'll find that all the cookies look identical, and it's possible they taste near identical. However, you'll also find all of them are labeled differently. That can be a really concerning thing for someone who shouldn't be eating something that's not safe for them, when another blanket calls all chocolate chip cookies from a package Chips Ahoy, even if they aren't.

Parties or special events can also feel kind of excluding for a child if they are not able to fully participate in the activities done. For example, there could be activities with foam stickers that really require intensive fine motor skills in order to peel off the paper backs. Perhaps it's gingerbread house making or 100th Day of School counting, where a child needs to be able to pick up small objects. It could also be a physical activity like a school Fun Run. Maybe your child cannot run or have the reward offered. How can they be accommodated so they can join in, (other than just raising money!) and have a good time?

It's important to let the school know as soon as you find out about this event, if they didn't tell you about it first, that there needs to be a way to include your child so they can participate and have fun. Perhaps it's having a few special buddies to walk along with your child on the Fun Run or perhaps it is sending a list of safe foods and brands home for parents to donate for the classroom snack with the teacher and school nurse each reading the labels to check.

There are a lot of things that can be done, but let's be honest, as well. There are times when schools do not want to accommodate. A teacher does not want to accommodate. It's too much work. The administration isn't supportive. They've too many students to worry about just one. Those are the times that you need to decide if you will fight for the inclusion or if you will simply walk away. There's no shame in either, and there's pride in standing for what you believe in, and what your child deserves, inclusiveness.

When that happens, if there's any way possible and it works for your schedule, I personally don't see anything wrong with keeping a child home that day. It's better to know that they can have a fun event planned with a grandparent or a parent or even a beloved babysitter, then to sit there and feel miserable and left out.

While by no means an ideal situation, inclusiveness is always preferred, it's hard for a child to see others having a good time while they aren't. It's something that lingers with them. I'm sure if you think about it, you can recall times that's happened to you, and it's a bit soul crushing. Advocating is all about the physical health and education deserved for your child, but it's also about making sure they are included.

27

FIELD TRIPS

Field trips are often, but not always entirely, the teacher's domain of power. Field trips are usually worked into the school standards of learning. Students might be visiting places that are connected to a particular unit of study, or a topic they need to cover.

While most children look forward to field trips, not all locations are required to accommodate those with special needs. Several years ago, you might recall a news story that went viral on a young girl who had a disability that required her to be in a wheelchair. Her class had planned their annual field trip to a state park. Instead of allowing her to be excluded, since a wheelchair wouldn't have been possible to use, her amazing teacher carried her the entire trip, and the girl was able to enjoy the day with her classmates.

Teachers like that are incredible. It really does go above and beyond, and I seriously bet that girl and her parents will always remember that moment of inclusiveness. Obviously, not all teachers can physically do such a thing, but perhaps there can be another way to practice inclusiveness. Your first stop is obviously the child's teacher. Most schools should have someone well versed in the ADA requirements and compliance. What can they do to help you? What kind of reasonable accommodation can be made?

Calling ahead to the field trip location can sometimes give guidance as to what aspects can and cannot be accommodated. For example, a field trip to a historic house might not be wheelchair accessible, but the grounds might be. Though a house tour might not be possible, could they bring activities or historical objects outside to allow all the children to participate in the learning? Are some areas accessible and a special guide available for the parts that aren't to tell stories or answer questions and show pictures?

A child with hearing loss might not be able to watch a video. If they are too young to be able to read closed captioning, will a sign language interpreter be available to help? For the child with asthma or diabetes who might require medicine to be given at certain times, who will carry the medicine, who will administer it and are they trained, and how will you be sure of your child getting it on time? Those are all great, and important, questions to ask.

Sometimes information about field trips is available at the start of school, particularly if the teacher has been doing the same trips for several years. That gives you time to start your own research, and create ideas of ways for your child to be included that school staff might not have thought of.

I'm going to stop here and add, I know. I know it's not fair that you have to work as hard as you do to keep your child included. It stinks. And it's not fair. But I also can promise you that if you keep doing it, if you keep fighting for your child's needs and inclusion with a positive attitude, and one of "let's work together" then changes for the better will happen.

The Americans with Disabilities Act and section 504 Plan of the Rehabilitation Act requires schools to provide reasonable accommodations for students who have physical or mental conditions so that they can have equal access to services and programs that their peers are given. This extends to field trips, class trips, clubs, and other school activities as well, so do not let the school say otherwise.

If your child does not have a 504 Plan, they should have one. You'll find this information repeated. *That's how important it is.* If your child's school tries to convince you they should have an IHP or IEP instead, you need to think carefully before agreeing. There are not the same protections given with an IEP or IHP. I'll explain more about what these are, and why your child might need one in an educational setting in a little. Just know that for field trips, if you have a 504 Plan, reasonable accommodations should be made.

28

LUNCHROOM

Advocacy in a lunchroom can be different scenarios. It's possible a child has a physical or mental disability that requires them to have assistance in opening packaging with their lunch. Perhaps they need a straw for their milk or might even need help to eat lunch. Advocacy also could be letting the school know your child needs a spot to eat their lunch away from certain allergens. It could also be sharing your child is physically unable to carry their lunch tray and needs someone to help them do that.

In the lunchroom, it's very important the staff are aware of your child's specific needs and how they can support your child. It's critical that the environment be one of support and kindness so a child does not feel embarrassed or awkward that they have a need others do not.

Sometimes staff members do not always approach these situations in the best way possible. They are busy. There are so many children they might struggle to remember who needs help and how. Or, just as in the case of others, it's likely that they have not even thought of these concerns. For example, a child with an allergy at a separate table. The teachers and lunchroom staff think it's not a big deal if the child sits at an allergen-free table. However, anything could be a food allergen. If a child with a dairy allergy sits down at the same spot a child with a nut allergy had just eaten a cheese sandwich and cheese crackers at, there could be a serious health risk, especially if the same rag was used to clean the table from one to the next, or crumbs remain on the table or seat.

On that same note, if a child needs someone to carry their tray to lunch, however, the person doesn't stay to open their milk or remove the packaging from a sandwich, then that's not helping the child. These needs and ways to meet those needs should be written into the IHP or 504 Plan, but just because it is written in, does not always mean that it is followed.

In some schools, children are rotated out to help wipe down the table after their class or sweep the floor. Is this something your child will need to do? Can they do so? This is another important thing to think about. It might be something you want to address before your child enters the school.

It's very important during meetings before the school year starts, and any time an issue arises and you have found out your child was excluded, to take the time to have another meeting with the school administration and anyone who comes into contact with your child to make sure that they are being treated how they need to be. Any sort of reasonable accommodation that could be made should be made. A child is no different for needing a little extra help in one area than another child is for needing help in another way. While many times classmates try and fill in and are incredibly helpful, it's not fair to them if an adult places the responsibility on a classmate to help open packages or to carry things when those children need to be able to have their full lunch time to eat as well.

Additionally, if something were to happen, like a lunch item spilling or an allergic reaction, it would not be right to blame a child when an adult should have been in charge of the situation and looking out for the one who needed their care. Here are some questions that you might want to ask as you're forming a plan for lunch:

- Does my child need to eat at a specific spot?

- Will the tables be wiped clean in between each person who sits there?

- How will the tables be wiped?

- Will there be anyone to help my child with carrying their tray or opening packaging?

- When it's time to clean up, what is my child expected to do?

29

BEFORE OR AFTER SCHOOL PROGRAMS

This information is primarily for those children who have medical needs. After school programs vary by school district. Some are run by school staff, others county or city employees, and still others outside programs. It doesn't matter which, but if your child is in one of these programs, you'll need to be sure they are taken care of. School sponsored or school led activities, including any after school program, are required to follow an IHP, IEP, or 504 Plan. However, if the school is not the one providing the program, they are not required to follow the same rules. This is when it will be very important to have a meeting before signing your child up. This is for two reasons, of course, your child's safety and inclusion being the first, but the second is financial. Often when paying for one of these programs, you do not get a full refund if you withdraw your child.

Things to ask any before or after school program would be:

- Are you CPR certified?

- Who here is trained to administer medicines, epipens, insulin, etc?

- Where are medicines and medical devices stored?

- How is the administration of a medical device tracked?

- Are parents informed at the time of an emergency?

- What are situations where food will be given?

- Will there be games or activities that my child might not be able to participate in?

As often these programs are primarily for childcare, education needs don't usually need to be addressed. If there are additional medical concerns that your child might need to have addressed, make a list and be sure that each adult there is aware of who your child is, what they need, how to take care of them, and how to reach you in an emergency.

30

SCHOOL WIDE EVENTS AND PTO / PTA

School wide events are often fundraisers and involve rewards. Many times, the prizes are things such as pizza or ice cream parties, movies, special assemblies, and the events things such as a fun run, field day, or other sort of physical activity.

Often the teacher doesn't have information about the event ahead of time, so you'll need to find out who does. For a Parent Teacher Organization (PTO) or Parent Teacher Association (PTA) sponsored event, check with them. If it's a school-sponsored event, you'll want to check in the school administrators.

If at all possible, it is important to become a part of the school PTO or PTA or at least attend the meetings. Not only will you have a heads up on events that are coming, you will also be able to have input to make it inclusive for everyone. Many volunteers do not understand that things are not inclusive for everyone. When something is a tradition and it has always been done that way, often we don't think of any other way to do it. Think about your own traditions. It's quite likely you make the same foods each year at Thanksgiving or Christmas. Perhaps you have the same birthday traditions in your home. Thinking about doing something different can sometimes feel uncomfortable, because you wonder, *what if it doesn't work out?* It's also likely that you, like the people putting on this event, use the same items year after year. It becomes a habit, but also one that you do because you already have the items or the plan.

This is when the fresh perspective, like that of a parent of a special needs child, can really benefit so many both now and in the future. Are there enough activities or rewards available so that if a child is not able to do one, they can still do the majority? Is there any way to make the event that they can't participate in inclusive so they can still have the fun of being with their friends? Will the food served or given as an incentive be able to be enjoyed by everyone? If not, can there be a similar alternative for those who need something different?

Focusing on and asking: "What way can we make it inclusive for everyone?" allows others to start brainstorming. For example, instead of ice cream, could snow cones be done? Does the reward even really need to be food? Instead of a school wide donuts and pizza party, could you do something else like give a special T-shirt or extra recess or a book to take home?

Many times, these event organizations are run by parents who want to be involved in their child's school and help raise funds to fill those gaps between government funding and student needs. I truly believe most of them do not intend to exclude anyone. Exclusion can happen because the need is not always recognized, especially when the parents of a child with additional needs do not help to plan the events. It can be busy and it can be overwhelming and it can be absolutely yes, one more thing you have to do. But generally, those meetings are held once a month for about an hour. By being a part of them, you can really make a difference.

Remember, your 504 Plan does carry over to school-sponsored events. If you find that even by trying to collaborate with the individuals running the organized event, you are not making any progress, remind your school administrator that reasonable accommodation needs to be made to include your child if the event is being held on school property or is associated with the school in any way.

31

EXTRACURRICULARS AND SPORTS

Extracurriculars and sports are a shared topic. Although not all extracurricular activities are held outside of school hours, during school hours there might be an activity where your child needs to be included. It might be a special activity such as a field trip or reward or fundraising activity. In those instances, it might be helpful to look at the field trips section or the PTO / PTA section.

It's also important to remember that accommodations given through a 504 Plan or an IHP may not extend to these extras, even those that are school sponsored. As I had mentioned earlier about FAPE, when it comes to sports or extracurriculars, it doesn't guarantee a spot in that activity or any special treatment. If this is a county or city or privately paid for extracurricular or sport, you also won't have these documents to help you, and it will all be based upon advocating, and hoping others help accommodate to include your child.

When it comes to sports, as they vary dramatically, it's helpful to first consider what it is your child would like to do. If it's an activity that is safe for them to participate in, identify any potential issues (limited mobility, immune concerns, contact reactions, etc.) and then ask the coach to help you think of a creative way for the child to still be included. Perhaps you have a child with a leg brace and they really want to play recreational baseball. They may not be able to play every single position, and if children rotate positions, there might be something they can't do, but is there something that they can do?

Perhaps your child wishes to do a sport, but it wouldn't be safe for them to do the ones typically offered by a school or county / city recreation department. Think outside the box. Would swimming, horseback riding, recreational gymnastics, yoga, or dance be an alternative? These are all sports that almost anyone can participate in. It might take a little research to find the place, but it's out there!

It's important to remember that just like in the PTO and PTA, many of these adults coaching the sports are volunteers. They want to be inclusive, they just don't always understand how. They are also just like you and me. Swamped with responsibilities and prone to forgetting things. They may not always, especially upon first meeting your child, remember what needs they have. It's your job, and your child's, to advocate in the mindset of working together, not working against.

However, on the note of food provided at sports. If that's a concern for your family, you do need to be aware parents who provide snacks may not be aware of your child's individual needs. There have been many stories in the food allergy community of parents who bring cupcakes or donuts for the end of a sporting game and several children not being able to eat them. The coach was aware of the allergy, but somehow that information didn't make it to the parents.

While the majority of sports teams have working together as the priority, be aware also that some children use sports as an opportunity to let out their aggressions. Perhaps they are too competitive, or maybe they just are using the sport as an opportunity to bully someone, but it does happen. If this does, you must take a firm stance. Bullying behavior is not something that should be tolerated, encouraged, or overlooked.

Sometimes you have to be unpopular to be heard. You have to speak up for your child's needs, and by doing so, you could be protecting another too scared to speak up, or opening a doorway for those to come forward with their own concerns, making the road easier for them to be heard.

While there will always be difficulties in groups, so many children are actually better at being inclusive and welcoming of other children than adults are! They are willing to do things differently so that everyone can join in. These children are incredibly caring, and good examples to all those around them. Sports can bring out the worst in some, but can bring out the best in many.

32

IHP, IEP, AND 504 PLANS INTRODUCTION

These have been mentioned several times throughout the book, and now is the time to explain what these are, and why they are so important. If your child is in school, they might need an Individual Health Plan (IHP), Individualized Education Program (IEP), or a 504 Plan. I'm going to tell you a little about each, so you are prepared when the school tries to offer one over another, and why you might or might not want to agree with that suggestion. As always, also please do your own research. This is just a highlight about what each of these is and you'll want to do a little more digging yourself.

As you research these sections, become familiar with the language used and the differences between each. When you talk to school staff, they will recommend one over the other based on how they see the situation. Remember, how the school staff sees your child's needs may not be how you see their needs. One of these will give you much more protection than the others. Only you, not the school, can be sure of what your child needs to be given when it comes to the proper documentation that will allow for the inclusiveness they deserve.

Each school district should have a 504 Plan coordinator. This is usually the person who also helps with the IEP or IHP. However, like anything else, consider that what they present for your child might be in the school's best interest, not your own. *Read everything carefully and ask all of your questions before you sign anything.*

As a reminder, I'd mentioned earlier how the Supreme Court established FAPE as part of the 1973 Rehabilitation Act and IDEA. It states that schools need to provide this free and appropriate education to all students. However, schools only need to show that students are making adequate progress. As I'd also explained, FAPE isn't limitless in its right to have. For example, this free and appropriate education doesn't require schools to provide the best services possible for students. It also doesn't require that each student's potential be maximized.

This is why having everything set in a document is so important.

Additionally, FAPE doesn't mean that schools have to offer a specific educational program, no matter how good it is, or even provide a specific class setting that a parent wants their child to have, even if it would be beneficial. This is why it's important to have the support of your school staff. Further, remember, when it comes to sports or extracurriculars, it also doesn't guarantee a spot in that activity or any special treatment. FAPE only requires schools to provide services that are considered to be reasonably calculated to help the student make progress.

As upsetting as it is, it's unrealistic to expect schools to tailor every aspect of the education world to a single student since they just have to do the minimum to ensure they can learn. This is why advocating, and having the proper plan set up for your child (IEP, IHP, or 504 Plan) is incredibly critical. The good news is, you don't have to do this alone.

There are advocates you can find locally or at a short distance away who will go in with you to help set up your IHP, IEP, or 504 Plan. Be aware that there may be a charge for some advocate services. These advocates are trained to help you cut through the red tape, know the phrases and language you need for results, and will even sit there with you ahead of time, crafting a perfect plan for your child. A simple Google, and then the word IHP, IEP, or 504 Plan will pull up multiple resources to get you started.

Now, let's learn the differences between each of these plans.

33

INDIVIDUAL HEALTH PLANS (IHP)

An Individual Health Plan (IHP) creates a plan to address what might happen medically while your child is in school. While the plan is intended to only address medical issues that don't have an effect on the child's learning, some things that cross over into the realm of education might be added in as safety protocols.

For example, my youngest son was given an IHP for his food allergies. In it, it stated he would be allowed to have his own water bottle to use instead of the water fountain, as well as own needed school supplies that could be kept at his desk, meaning he would not have to use shared pencils, markers, etc. It also stated that the teacher would notify, if possible, seventy-two hours before food was to be used in lessons to allow for a substitute to be brought in by me, and that he was to be allowed an adult cleaned table at lunch.

Now...let me interrupt myself to say that while an IHP is supposed to be a formal agreement that outlines the needs and a plan for addressing those needs, it is NOT legally binding. If a mistake happens, well, there's no legal recourse. Which is why very often a school will insist that an IHP is what's needed, not a 504 Plan, and why it is so hard to get that 504, as it was in our case. One more thing about an IHP. It can be *combined* with a 504 Plan, especially if the 504 Plan doesn't cover everything medically. Remember that. It's possible to have both. In your child's specific situation, it might even be encouraged.

The IHP is put together jointly by the child's caregiver, the child's doctor, and the staff at the school, usually the school nurse and possibly a disability coordinator. This is meant to be a tool, a plan, for parents or other caregivers, doctors, and school staff to work together to keep the child healthy. In the plan it discusses *what* needs to be done, and *who* is responsible for doing that thing.

As another example, if your child needs medication during the day, the IHP might say where the medicine will be located and how it will be stored, what plan there is to administer the medicine, and the frequency of doses. There might even be something about the parents' responsibility to make sure the medicine supply doesn't run low.

Usually, the IHP gets reviewed and signed off on each year by the school nurse or other staff, and the parent. It should also follow the child from one school to the next in the same district, but please check with your school about that. The IHP can also be changed if something needs to be updated, however, you will need all the previous parties involved to help with that change and sign off on the new changes.

Now, remember how I said there's no protection or recourse if the IHP isn't followed? This is important. Don't forget this part. That's because an IHP isn't given any state or federal protection. IHP's are developed by school districts.

That was a lot of info. Let's do a quick refresher. Who needs an IHP?

- Any child who has a health condition

- Any child who has a disability that's physical (as in, could cause a physical problem to the child's health)

What does the IHP do?

-

It documents the services or accommodations needed

- It provides a way for school staff and parents to team up to protect the child

Even if your child has a condition but medicine or a medical device isn't likely to be administered at school, (think diabetes, or a feeding tube, or a colostomy bag) it is important to have the IHP so the teacher and all school staff know how to deal with any emergencies that might come up. When there is a medical condition, there is always the possibility of an emergency situation. This information could also be helpful to emergency responders in the event they are needed.

When creating the IHP, make sure you are involved in each step, and that your voice and your child's needs are covered and documented. Make sure everything is signed. Be sure nothing is left out. You should be allowed to request reasonable accommodations and expect that the school will follow through. If need be, get a letter from your child's doctor requesting them.

However, remember, there is no legal binding with an IHP. That's why we are moving next onto the 504 Plan, the legally binding, harder to get plan for your child.

34

The 504 Plan

So, what is this 504 Plan I keep talking about? A 504 Plan is a *legally binding agreement* between the legal guardian and the school district. This is why it's the gold standard, and the thing you really want for your child. A 504 Plan is a part of the Americans with Disabilities Act (ADA). That means there are consequences if it's not followed.

Children who have disabilities that do not interfere with their ability to progress in general education are not eligible for special education services. However, they may be entitled to the protection provided by a 504 Accommodation Plan. And that's what you want, that protection. The legally binding document that is taken seriously. 504 Plans are used for various things, meaning they can cover a single concern or several.

504 Plans typically will address accommodations in academic areas, but there is spillover if those unmet accommodations in the academic need could affect a child's health. For example, if a child isn't given THIS accommodation, then the result of THAT could happen, which would affect their ability to be in school, or progress with their peers educationally.

These plans can also be applied to nonacademic areas and extracurricular activities, so that the student can have a similar whole school experience as their peers. The 504 Plan can follow the student to college and is also applicable in the workplace.

Oddly enough, despite being legal documents, 504 Plans are not as involved as an IEP. It also does not cover all of the things in one. A 504 Plan should talk about staff training and specify who will provide that training. The plan should also include review dates so that the plan can remain current and address all of your child's needs.

Now, how to get one of these plans? A 504 Plan can be requested by either you or school personnel. Together, the legal guardian and a team of school staff work up the plan. Usually, this would be the administrator and a coordinator, or case manager. Sometimes if the issues addressed in the 504 Plan are related to a medical condition, the treating medical providers are also included in setting up the plan.

You've heard me mention this 504 plan over and over, so you might be wonder...does my child need one of these? Here are some general guidelines for that. If your child's medical needs significantly limit one or more major life activities, including school, then he or she *should* have a 504 Plan. What could severely limit them? That's for *you* to say, not the school. You know your child's health and what struggles they may have. How would those struggles impact their education if this or that happened? Think about a child with chronic fatigue, or Crohn's disease. Schoolwork could be affected because they might not be able to attend a full day of school, and might have more absences than another child. For those reasons, or any reason where medical issues could impact education, you might need to see about getting the 504 Plan.

The goal of a 504 Plan is to provide a level playing field by making accommodations and modifications to allow the student the same opportunities as their "typical" peers. Having this plan also is a form of advocating, because it almost forces inclusiveness, by law, if you are getting pushback from school staff. This plan puts the responsibility on the school staff. Maybe these accommodations are for a tutor or more time allotted on things. Perhaps it's for a quiet place to work. Whatever your child needs to succeed is what you ask for.

Before a 504 Plan meeting, think of what your child might need while he or she is at school, and what accommodations your child might require to meet those needs. Have it all written down in advance so you've had plenty of time to review it and not miss anything and you don't get rattled or talked over. See the Communication section, if you need a refresher.

Once they've agreed to give you a 504 Plan, what things are in it? The plan can include adaptive equipment or assistive technology devices, an aide, assistance with health-related needs, different school transportation, or other services and accommodations your child needs for educational success.

Remember, it is your right to have a 504 Plan, but so many schools argue against it. Instead, they may tell you an IHP or IEP is all that's needed. As the expert in such things, don't you automatically assume they are correct and know what's best? You aren't experienced in this, so you might just agree and give in. However, that might not be the right choice for your child. *I've repeated this because it's so important. Unless you have a 504 Plan, it's not a legally binding plan or document and does not hold the school responsible to provide inclusion.*

Phew, that was a lot of info. Let's do a quick refresher. Who needs a 504 Plan?

- Any child who has a condition that might impact their education

What does the 504 Plan do?

- It legally binds the school district to provide special accommodations

35

INDIVIDUALIZED EDUCATION PROGRAM (IEP)

This is the last plan that might be mentioned for your child. An Individualized Education Program (IEP) is generally for those students who have documented gaps in learning. The IEP is developed to address these gaps. However, an IEP can also be used when a potential gap is anticipated, such as a child who may experience difficulty staying on top of classwork due to frequent illness and absences, or a child whose hearing impairment or emotional disturbance necessitates there be modifications and / or accommodations in the curriculum.

This *is* a legally binding document based on the Individuals with Disabilities Education Act (IDEA).

IDEA ensures services to children with disabilities throughout the nation. The rules for IEPs are set out by the federal government, and states then have to implement these rules. However, as some states may interpret the federal mandates differently, IEPs are not always going to be the same from state to state, even states that touch borders where people commonly live and work in two different states, such as Virginia and West Virginia or Maryland and Washington D.C. This means that if your child moves from one state to the next, you may need to start the IEP process over, quite possibly even testing, and the outcome might be different (good or bad) from what they had earlier.

An interesting thing with IEPs is that they give you backing and guaranteed procedural safeguards. They also call for mandatory progress reports. Those are beneficial for both you and the school to ensure that your child is getting the best education they can get.

Now, how do you know if this is the best plan for your child? If your child has a condition or disability that interferes with or impacts their ability to learn and makes it where they can't succeed in their education without these modifications to the regular curriculum, they may qualify.

If it seems as though this might be the plan that your child needs, you can ask that they be evaluated for an IEP. A caregiver isn't the only one who can ask for this evaluation. Anyone, such as a teacher or school administrator, can also ask for the evaluation. They cannot and will not do this without you, though. The legal guardian must be involved in the process from referral, assessment, and planning to develop the IEP.

After the initial evaluation, and if your child is granted the IEP, they must also undergo another evaluation every three years. This is not an optional thing. IEP reviews are mandated by law. However, if you feel as though you need one sooner, you can request a more frequent review. The benefit of this is if the IEP is not working well, then it can be revised. That's important, and a great thing to do.

What might need to be revised? Typically, IEPs provide modifications to curriculum and accommodations in instructional methods or materials, including the class assignments and assessments, and time allotted to complete them. These accommodations also exist for standardized testing days. During state testing, accommodations can be given to extended time or allow additional restroom breaks.

What if you aren't happy with the IEP? Ideally, before the IEP is finalized, you've voiced your concern. This is where you need to advocate for your child if you are not happy with parts of the IEP. Also, you do not need to sign the IEP until you all come to an agreement about what it says. The legal guardian is the one who must approve the IEP, including what accommodations are on it, the frequency of services, and anything else there. The school will not be able to change anything without your permission. Any changes or updates wanted on the IEP must be approved by you.

Let's do a quick refresher and hit the bullet points. Who needs an IEP?

- Any child who has an educational concern

- Any child who has a disability that requires them to have modifications or accommodations to learn

What does the IEP do?

- It documents the services, modifications, or accommodations needed

- It provides a way for school staff and parents to work together to provide the education a child needs

36

WHEN IT'S JUST NOT WORKING AT SCHOOL

There might come a time when you feel like it's not working at school. You've tried advocating. You tried for the IEP, IHP, 504 Plan and everything else, but no matter what you do, it's not working. The broken things can't be fixed. Emotions are running high, your child isn't getting the help or attention they need, and it's become a stressful and upsetting situation for everyone.

There are many reasons for this, and it's not always any one person's fault. Maybe you've realized that the traditional classroom setting just isn't nourishing your child in the way they need. It could be there are problems at the school that can't be solved, or that your family is experiencing a crisis of some sort at home and your child needs to be taken care of by you, not the school. For many with complex or chronic medical needs, schools simply will not work with the parents to allow children time they need to recover and heal and visit doctors without pushing them to return to school and stay on top of things when they physically cannot.

What are your options? There are four ideas to consider.

- A different school within the district

- Private schools

- Online schools

- Homeschool

Things get a little complicated if your child has specific needs and they had been getting services from the school district. While you will need to look into this more, once a problem is identified and documented, some states allow those services to continue in a home setting if going a virtual school or homeschool route. Insurance might also cover these services, or they could be available online. Perhaps you've even decided to take over that role yourself. Just know that there are options.

I'm the first to understand that finances can be tight. It's possible private school isn't an option. Homeschool might not be possible if there isn't an adult able to stay home during the day. However, I'm going to talk a little about each, and you might be surprised at how possible any of these options are for your child.

37

A DIFFERENT SCHOOL WITHIN THE DISTRICT

This is likely to be the first and easiest option. You don't automatically have to assume that you'll need to move neighborhoods. Attending a school that's different from your zoned area is fairly commonplace. Often school districts allow a child to go to a different school. There are multiple reasons that they might let that happen. The first is if a parent works for the school district or works closer to that school. Another is if their needs are not being met at one school and the services are being offered at another. One more reason is if there's been a very serious issue with another student or teacher.

Now, there are plenty of families who have definitely moved and switched neighborhoods to get into a different school district. Absolutely nothing wrong with that, however, it is worth exploring getting permission before you consider an expensive and time-consuming activity like packing and moving, especially because what if you go to all of that trouble, and it's not a better situation?

According to greatschools.org, a quarter of kids go to a school that they are not zoned for. While admissions processes can be complicated, it is not impossible. Speak with someone in your county administration office if you do not feel comfortable talking with your child's current administrator. It does not hurt to have multiple reasons for why you want to enroll your child in that school. While you definitely can bring up things like wanting access to better services, don't be afraid to mention things like it's closer to your home or your work than the school that you are zoned for, or even bullying. Perhaps that school is a nut free school for your child with food allergies and you want to be there.

Give solid reasons, keep calm, and use the tips that I share and the section titled Conversations. Remember the importance of writing things down. You want to make sure that you are documenting things and communicating in a way that will get you the best outcome.

The biggest problem with switching schools is often transportation is not available for your child, so that is something important to consider.

38

PRIVATE SCHOOL

With more private schools popping up, it's likely that your child cannot only get a smaller student to-teacher ratio, but also still get the same kind of help and attention that they need in order to thrive in a classroom setting. I know the first thing most people think about when they hear the words private school is cost. It is true that you do have to pay at a private school because the majority of them do not receive government funds.

However, what many people do not realize is that most private schools have some sort of scholarship program. These scholarships can greatly reduce the cost of the education tuition. The best way to find out if your child would be eligible is to contact the school. It's likely someone there can help you and make suggestions or even point you over to a different school that would have a scholarship available for your child.

One thing to be aware of is with a private school, an IEP or 504 Plan may not be an option if the school does not receive any government funding.

39

Online Schools

While online school has been around for quite a while, it was not until the coronavirus pandemic that most children were exposed to them in one form or another. Whether it was from a school district offering their own version or the students were transferred over to an online school, most of us realized suddenly that there were *other options*.

The thing about an online school for a caregiver is that you know your child will have a teacher and be given assignments. It's very much as if they were in school, yet the lessons are taught remotely. That means if you have a workplace that allows your child to go with you, your child can be there with you while still in school. Or the child can learn from home (if someone is there with them) or a relative's house. In an area where multiple children are using the same online learning system, you might even be able to form a group where the classes are all held in one central location where an adult can take turns keeping an eye on the children to make sure they are doing their work and that help is there if any needs arise.

There are some fantastic options for online schooling. There are both public and private school options. Some have no charge at all, while others charge a little, and still others, a full private school price. Research will reveal many more options for online schooling that you could have imagined, if that's the desired route for your child.

40

HOMESCHOOLING

What's the first thing you think of when you hear homeschooling? There seems to be a stigma attached (Your child won't ever socialize! They're just going to watch TV all day!) and a feeling others like to project that just because you are not a teacher you will not be able to give your child a good education.

I find the idea absolutely ridiculous. What parent or caregiver has not already been the child's first teacher? Chances are very good that you have taught your child many things. Their colors, the names of objects and people and food. How to become toilet trained and how to put their clothing on. Now, you might be thinking, of course! But I don't know how to describe a predicate when it comes to English class. And I certainly don't know algebra! And that very well may be true. But I bet you are good at letting your fingers do the walking online to browse around different pre-made homeschooling curriculums.

There is an absolute wealth of both paid and free resources for homeschooling your child. If you want to put together a curriculum from scratch, customizing it to your child and their interests while still meeting state standards you absolutely can. If you would rather buy curriculum with lessons already planned that you just read and teach, you can do that as well. You'll even find that many of these pre-made curriculums also have video lessons to go along with them, and teachers you can call if you or your child get stuck.

Additionally, you will find a great number of these are practically hands off. Many homeschooling curriculums were created by parents who have multiple children in multiple grades and understand the need to have these bundles put together so that a child can simply work on it.

41

WHAT'S THE BEST ALTERNATE SCHOOL CHOICE?

What you read was only a short overview of alternatives, but it shows you have options. Something you might not have even known is possible! But, with these new possibilities presenting themselves, which is the right one?

The best choice is the one that works for your personal needs and is what's best for your child. If a traditional public school environment is not working, then take a little time to analyze why it is not working for your child. Do they thrive in that structured setting, but the environment is not conducive to learning? Are they not getting the educational help and resources that they should have? Perhaps switching schools or moving to a private school is what they need. On the other hand, if your child does well learning on their own and the environment in the school has become such that your child dreads that traditional school setting, of there is a health concern and an in person classroom just isn't possible to keep your child learning, online school or homeschooling might be a good option.

Sometimes we must choose these other ways in order to advocate for our child and see that their needs—all of their needs—are met. Remember, it's not just your child's education. It's also their mental wellbeing, their physical wellbeing, and their emotional wellbeing that need care as well.

The important thing to remember is that *you are not failing your child* by taking them from a public school. You are more than capable as an adult to educate your child if you choose to homeschool. One of the best things about an alternative school method is that often your child has an opportunity to go more in depth on a subject that interests them. With online schools and homeschooling, there can be supplemental learning added as well. If your child is interested in Egyptian mythology, they can have that time they want to explore that topic more. They don't need to just memorize something for the sake of passing a test. They can actually go deeper and enjoy what they love to learn about.

I had mentioned briefly that if your child is receiving some sort of educational services that there is a possibility they still can continue if you choose an alternative method of schooling. One thing to note is that not all private schools have those services available because often they are paid for by taxpayer dollars. Some private schools do, but that is something that you would need to check into.

There are always options to get the help your child needs. This is one of those times you may have to weigh the benefit versus the cost of getting those services. It might be that you have to drive a little bit to get to them or you cannot have those services at home. However, you will not know unless you start asking around and making phone calls.

On a last note, sometimes parents remove their children to homeschool and at a later time return their children to public school. There's nothing wrong with that either. You might not know what works best for your child until you try an alternative option.

PART FOUR

Family and Friends

42

FAMILY AND FRIENDS

This is the last section, and the smallest. It's quite tiny, I won't lie, because I'm giving advice about relationships. I wanted to include it though, because there might be times you need to advocate for your child with family or friends. There could be situations you are in and feel uncomfortable about. Think of this as one last pep talk.

We can love our family, we can love our friends. That doesn't mean that they know everything, and it sure doesn't mean that they know what's best for our child.

As you read, remember that, and that just like in other situations, it's okay to walk away if you need to.

43

FAMILY

Family. Family can be hard. It's my experience that family falls into one of three categories. First, there's the questioning and disbelieving family members. They are the ones walking around saying, "Are you sure? Nobody in my family ever had anything like this before." They are pretty set and firm in their opinion that because they've never seen that, it doesn't exist or doesn't matter or you are exaggerating.

Then there's also the excluding sort. The ones who don't want to invite you to anything because they're concerned about your child's diagnosis. They're worried about that diagnosis rubbing off on them somehow or they simply don't want to make any sort of accommodation, no matter how small, whatsoever. That can be a difficult thing for your child, who, through no fault of their own, wonders why this family member never wants to be around them.

Finally, the third type I observe are the well-meaning and well-intentioned individuals who genuinely do want to help your child, but perhaps don't know how. This category can be further broken down into two subsections. Those who learn and wholeheartedly embrace your child as they are and those who honestly admit that they don't know what to do and so they want to leave that up to you. They'll help, but they need you to be specific on how. Or else they are truthful that they simply cannot accommodate.

Believe it or not, that's the kind of person I actually prefer. If you cannot accommodate my child or if you don't feel comfortable providing him a way to be included, I would prefer to know that up front. It won't hurt my feelings, even if it hurts theirs, but it lets me know that you understand how serious how important this situation is and that you don't feel up to the responsibility. Who could be upset at someone for admitting that? It takes a brave person to admit when they can't do something or don't know how. We need to celebrate and appreciate these people.

There will be times that you find yourself around family, perhaps during holidays or special occasions, and there's a situation that might come up. What are some ways that you can make sure your child is included and, if need be, advocate for them? You know your child best and you know what they need. It's important, obviously, that you have as much notice as possible before an event. Ask as many questions as you can.

For example, what kind of things will be done? Are there activities, games, or sports? The more you know ahead of time, the more you can help plan so that there is inclusiveness for your child. Maybe your child can't play the games or sports, maybe you don't feel comfortable with them eating the food. Maybe you know without an absolute shadow of doubt they should not be left alone with grandpa or Uncle Jeff or your sister Marie. All things that if you know ahead of time, you can plan and make accommodations for and find a way for your child to be included.

Because family gatherings are often with a very diverse group of people, sometimes this works well in your favor for inclusiveness. What I mean by that is if you are concerned your child will not be able to be part of the festivities, why not bring some of those festivities? Simple supplies, such as crayons and paper, and stickers or foam sheets provide enjoyment for multiple ages. Children love to make things and that lets your child feel included that something they can do others are enjoying as well. You could also even bring something simple, like a favorite DVD or a few toys that allow for open-ended play, like balls or LEGOs.

There's another alternative, and that's as much as possible to be in control of the situation. One of the largest things that our family needs inclusion on and advocacy for is food. So, as much as possible we try to host. When there is an event and we cannot host, we ask, what can we bring? We are very clear and up front on our children's needs. We also say, "Please don't be offended if we pack them their own food. Sometimes they are more comfortable eating something familiar they know mom prepared." Never once have we had anyone say anything about that. Who wouldn't want their guests to feel comfortable and at ease even if the food is slightly different?

The same goes for restaurants. Obviously, if there's some sort of a food situation that's an issue for your family you'll want to check ahead of time. If your child has mobility needs, that's also something that needs to be taken into consideration. It's surprising the number of restaurants that somehow do not have accommodations for those with disabilities. Frequently, I still see restaurants with steps and no ramp or chairs with arms instead of those without. There are tables packed close together and no room for a wheelchair or someone with a walker to navigate through.

Those are all things that need to be taken into consideration, whether with family or by yourself. No doubt about it, having a child with any sort of an additional need is extra work. But it's something that we do willingly and lovingly and happily because we want them to have the same experiences that others get to have. There is truly nothing better than seeing your child's face light up when they get to enjoy things with those they love.

This kind of experience does not come naturally for many families, though. If being around your family is more hurtful, stressful, and dangerous than it is worth, perhaps it is time to embrace your own over the top family celebrations and time together, within your household, and open your doors only to those who you want to invite in.

That might look something like saying you can't join the family on Thanksgiving, but Mom and Dad, you are invited that weekend for refreshments and time to visit. It could also be taking Aunt Susan out for dinner to celebrate her 60th birthday, but skipping her party. It is also possible if you explain to these people as to why you are doing that, they will understand.

You may find these smaller visits more enjoyable and less stressful anyway. A smaller get together also allows for more quality time and less chance of conflict. Always a win!

44

FRIENDS

Friends come in the adult age and the childhood age. So, I'm going to be splitting this up into two sections. Your child's friends and your friends. Obviously, children need to be handled differently and spoken too differently than an adult, however, there may be times the things you say could be the same.

45

YOUR CHILD'S FRIENDS

I hope that your child has good friends. I hope they have the kind that look after them and are willing to do anything for them. Sure, squabbles happen, but I mean the kind of friend you know has your back no matter what. Kids seem to have those more than adults do. Maybe it's because they need that, especially if one child has a medical need. My youngest child is blessed with two such friends, though they don't see each other as often as they'd like. They've been together for several years and one in particular is extremely protective of him. This little boy's mom goes above and beyond. She protects him and treats him just as if he was her own, and I cannot tell you how much that means to me.

He also has friends who he gets along with who see exclusion as not a big deal. They will go on ahead and do something that he cannot and not think twice about it. They will invite him, say to a birthday party, knowing that he cannot participate fully. Fortunately, at this point my son has not been bullied for his medical problems. I know that it can happen and it does happen often to other children. That is why it is so important to let your child know that it's okay to tell an adult and it's okay to stand up for yourself and that you don't need to always be polite about it.

I think for many of us who raise well-spoken and well-behaved children, they have learned not to interrupt an adult and they have learned that you try and get along with others. There is a time and a place though, for standing up for yourself. Being loud or being assertive is important and needed.

When it comes to friends, they've been taught since kindergarten it's important to be around friends who make you feel good and friends who make you feel happy. A person who says they are your friend but then does things to make you upset is not really a friend. Sometimes children need reminders of that. It is important that your child learn to recognize certain behaviors so when they do pop up, your child can assess the situation and decide if that is something that they are going to let slide (was a friend playing around and being silly) or was that something serious that needs to be handled by an adult or spoken against.

With friends, there are also boundaries that might need to be set. Perhaps you don't feel comfortable letting your child travel without you or having sleepovers. Be sure your child understands the reason, and speak with the other parents as well. It's much better to be up front: This is why we don't this thing, rather than just continuing to say no, and have them wonder why you always give that response.

By setting boundaries or having limitations it actually allows your child to feel safe. They know expectations and, if feeling pressured, have an easier time self-advocating when they know the rules.

46

YOUR FRIENDS

Adult friends can be tricky. You've got those who are genuinely concerned and helpful, those who don't care, and those falling in the middle, concerned and wanting to be a support but already overwhelmed and reeling with their own challenges. It's really the kind in the second category you need to watch for. A friend who can't at least support you on occasion, or speaks negatively about you, your child, or your challenges isn't a friend. Right? Isn't that what we would tell our kids? Yet so many of us allow this toxic behavior when it comes to who we associate with.

Remember that you are setting an example for your child as to how relationships of any kind should be. Also remember, you don't deserve to have people around you that cause hurt. Just as you are advocating for your child, remember it's okay to do that for yourself, as well.

PART FIVE

Final Words... When to Say Goodbye

47

WALKING AWAY

Sometimes you simply have to walk away. Walk away from a family member or from a longtime friend. Walk away from that toxic person who is not supportive, but instead hurtful. The person who potentially puts your child at risk or sucks every bit of joy from your soul. The school that refuses to help your child, the doctor who doesn't take you seriously.

You know you need to walk away.

Yes. It's difficult to do that. it's not like you can just pick up your house and move it away to get away from a neighbor. It's certainly very difficult to cut ties with someone you are related to. Perhaps you aren't sure what will happen if you remove your child from school, or how you are going to find a better doctor.

Remember, there is nothing wrong with putting your child and their needs first when you are in a situation that is causing harm. Today, we are so surrounded in this instant gratification world of Facebook likes and Amazon Prime two-day shipping that we lose patience. We've lost respect for each other. We don't accommodate those who need it. We hide behind screen names and leave nasty comments on news articles thinking, who cares? No one's going to see it and it's not going to hurt anyone, but I had an opportunity to be unkind.

The problem is, people do see those. Some people take great joy in the fact that their comments hurt others and there are some who simply can't help but read these comments, even if they know better. They might be hoping for glimpses of kindness, but instead they get hurt very deeply. It's important to know it's okay to walk away, and there are situations where you should walk away. This is likely one of them.

There are times that you need to remove that person from your social media or you simply need to stop answering phone calls or text messages. Blocking features are fantastic. If you feel like you need some sort of closure, then just tell the individual why you are removing yourself from the situation: "You've not been supportive," and "I'm not interested whatsoever in continuing to allow that kind of harm to my family". That's a hard thing to do or say, and you might just prefer to never tell them anything.

Just sort of fade away. Whatever is best for you. But if you are in a relational situation of any sort that causes you pain, and there's no support, then walk away. It might be the best thing for you. Can't walk away fully? Take a break, and reassess after a few months. How do you feel now?

When it's online and it's someone that you don't know, it's even easier to end the relationship. Stop reading the comments, stop looking at things, and stop replying. Don't even try and get into those social media arguments, even if you feel justified or defensive. You won't win. Facts, logic, reason? None of that matters to these people who only want to use their words to hurt others. It's a type of bullying and they enjoy making you upset.

Don't ever apologize for looking after your child's needs in any capacity. You are their protection. Their defense. Their advocate. That's your role.

Now, go be it unapologetically. You can do this.

Thank you for taking the time to read *The Unapologetic Advocate*

Could I ask for one small favor? Reviews like yours on Amazon mean so much to me and help others to find my books! Thank you for supporting indie authors!

Stop by my website to see everything I've written and keep up to date!

www.sarahlambbooks.com

Sarah Lamb is the mother of two boys and wife to a teacher. She spends her days writing and editing books in the beautiful Shenandoah Valley. Sarah loves nothing more than high-quality books that both entertain and open the reader's mind, allowing them to dream, and then later make those dreams come to life.

.

www.ingramcontent.com/pod-product-compliance
Lightning Source LLC
LaVergne TN
LVHW051052080426
835508LV00019B/1831